GETTING INTO PROGRAMMING-1

PROGRAMMING GUIDE

MAYANK'KASANA

I am a student of 9th standard Evergreen Public School, Delhi. I am also a programmer of python and a learner too as I have made this to give you a brief in relation to scratch and basic python programming, this is the booklet by which you can easily learn some coding fundamentals.

My teachers help me out in all this I face many barrier to print this outstanding thing.

My gratitude to you for all you have done, which I will never forget. I truly appreciate you and your time you spent helping me in many occasions.

Thank you very much for the course. I enjoyed every minute of your lecture as well as your marvelous sense of humor.

Thanks to my parents also who suppoeted me very much.

Contents

GETTING INTO PROGRAMMING (COLOUR EDITION) LET'S GO

Kasana Enterprises

WEBSITE

Thanks

Foreword

This is a complete booklet that contains all the basic coding like block code, script code, etc. you can learn all the fundamentals of this field .this book includes the installation, explanation, definition, examples, tables, theory, assignment, projects, and many more. You can start your programming carrier by completing this you will be one step closer to being professional and experienced in this field. Enjoy Learning!.....

Preface

This is a basic booklet here to guide you and learn about programming which is become a essential thing for our life. You will be getting

Projects

Theory

Samples

Suggestion

Pro-tips

How to start

And many more..

This book is about how to write code that's highly readable. The key idea in this book is that code should be easy to understand. Specifically, your goal should be to minimize the time it takes someone else to understand your code.

This book explains this idea and illustrates it with lots of examples from different languages, including C++, Python, and Scratch. We've avoided any advanced language features, so even if you don't know all these languages, it should still be easy to follow along. (In our experience, the concepts of readability are mostly language-independent, anyhow.)

Each chapter dives into a different aspect of coding and how to make it "easy to understand."

Acknowledgements

Mrs.Neelam, content helper

Mrs.Meenu'Gupta, error checker

Mrs.Shweta Gujral, a supporter

Mrs.Sunnaina'kappor, project helper

Miss.Prekshi,supporter

Miss.Shailjha,supporter

Mrs.Shruti, a supporter

Mrs.Noopur, helped to give that fuel to bring this book

Mrs.Deepshika, a supporter

Mr.Ansh'Jain, marketing, and mentor

@Rajesh'Kumar for support

And my family to allow me for this all and giving support

Some content is taken by:@Fred L. Drake, Jr., the creator of the original Python documentation toolset and writer of much of the content; @the Docutils project for creating reStructuredText and the Docutils suite; @Fredrik Lundh for his Alternative Python Reference project from which Sphinx got many good ideas.

Prologue

This is a guide to give a basic introduction to Scratch a visual programming language that allows students to create their own interactive stories, games, and animations. As students design Scratch projects, they learn to think creatively, reason systematically, and work collaboratively Python is a dynamic, interpreted (bytecode-compiled) language. There are no type declarations of variables, parameters, functions, or methods in the source code. This makes the code short and flexible, and you lose the compile-time type-checking of the source code.You can procced to start your book now or continue reading. This contains many things like all the materials as examples,codes,operations,project,logics,tips this is only a basic guide to become a good programmer instead to be a struggling programmer who eevrytimes waits to get online free videos to learn about the platform but here you will get the best and sorted guide to bulid your intrest in this field.

GETTING INTO PROGRAMMING (COLOUR EDITION) LET'S GO

GET INTO PROGRAMMING

BY-MAYANK'KASANA

Kasana Enterprises

GET INTO PROGRAMMING

KASANA ENTERPRISES

Lt.Sh.Ajay Pal Kasana

Sh.Raj Singh Kasana

Sachin kasan,Satish kasana

Mayank'kasana,Ayan'kasana

WEBSITE

https://mayankkasana038.wixsite.com/kasanaenterprises

SCAN

Thanks

EVERGREEN PUBLIC SCHOOL

A great teacher is a treasure to students, parents, and the community. Express your appreciation to excellent educators with a card of thanks – shared online, texted, or printed and posted.
Choose a message that suits this teacher, not just any teacher. What qualities, abilities, or character traits stand out? If your knowledge of the person is limited, elevate a generic "thank you" with a comment that's true of every good teacher, such as "The example you set of a strong, capable, loving adult is a real gift to children. Thank you." Most of all, follow through on your good intentions. A few words of gratitude lift and encourage, but not if we never send them.
THANKS

CHAPTER ONE

Introduction to scratch

Welcome to Scratch Programming for Teens! Scratch is a programming language developed by the MIT Media Lab for teaching programming to teens and other first-time programmers. Scratch is a new programming language, initially released in May 2007. Scratch supports the development of computer games, interactive stories, graphic artwork and computer animation, and all sorts of other multimedia projects. Scratch allows new programmers to create programs by snapping together blocks. Scratch consists of a programming language made up of different blocks and an easy-to-learn graphical development environment that includes a paint application for creating graphics and built-in sound editing capabilities. Scratch also comes with huge collections of sample applications as well as graphics and sound files, all of which you can use to create your Scratch projects. Scratch programs are made up of graphical blocks, which are snapped together. Scratch blocks resemble puzzle pieces in the way that they snap together. Scratch blocks can only be snapped together in ways that make sense, preventing new programmers from using them in invalid combinations. In this way, Scratch enforces proper programming syntax and ensures that new programmers learn the proper way to assemble and formulate programming logic. Scratch's development was inspired by the method that hip-hop DJs use to mix and scratch records to create new and unique music. In Scratch, new programmers can create new application projects that incorporate pre-built code blocks, graphics, and sound files in all kinds of new combinations. Scratch lets programmers modify applications on the fly, allowing changes to be made even while Scratch applications are running. The result is an interactive, real-time programming environment that encourages experimentation and learning. This book's primary goal is to teach you everything you need to know to learn the basics of computer programming with Scratch. To help accomplish this goal, this book will emphasize learning by doing through the development of a series of fun and interesting exercises.

Why Scratch?

Scratch provides everything needed to begin developing computer games, multimedia presentations, interactive stories, graphic artwork, and computer animation. Scratch can be used to play digital music and sound effects. Scratch's building block approach to programming sets it apart from other programming languages. This makes Scratch easier to learn. And yet Scratch provides plenty of programming power, allowing you to build very powerful application projects. If you aspire to one day become a professional programmer, you will find that Scratch provides everything needed to build a foundation from which you can make the transition. Scratch also packs all of the programming power and punch needed to satisfy the programming needs of most computer enthusiasts and hobbyists.

Who Should Read This Book?

Scratch Programming for Teens is designed to provide all of the instruction that a first-time programmer requires to quickly get up and running. Previous programming experience will certainly be helpful, but it is by no means a requirement of this book. This book makes no assumptions about your computer background other than that you are comfortable working with one of the operations systems supported by Scratch. This book provides everything you need to get started with Scratch. Before you know it, you will be creating all kinds of projects, incorporating graphics, sound, and animation. As you learn how to program with Scratch, you will learn programming principles and techniques that you can later apply to other programming languages. As such, you will be able to apply what you learn about programming with Scratch to other programming languages like Microsoft Visual Basic and AppleScript. What You Need to Begin Obviously, the first thing you need is a copy of Scratch. Scratch is available for free download at the Scratch website located at http://scratch.mit.edu/ download. You can also download a copy from the CD included in the back of the book. You also need good instruction, which you will find in this book. In addition to Scratch and this book, you need a computer running a supported operating system, which also meets Scratch's minimum system requirements. Supported Operating Systems Scratch can be run on computers using either Microsoft or Macintosh operating systems. Specifically, Scratch can be installed on a computer running any of the operating systems.

All of the figures and examples in this book will be shown using Scratch 1.2.1 running on computers using either Microsoft Vista or Mac OS X 10.5. If you are going to be working with Scratch on a different version of Windows or Mac OS X, you may notice small differences in the way things look. However, all major Scratch features and functionality should work the same and you should not have any problems following along with the instruction provided in this book.

Minimum System Requirements Scratch

does not impose any additional hardware requirements over and above those required by the operating system. However, as Table A.1 shows, Scratch does impose screen resolution and disk space requirements, which must be met for Scratch to run. To work with Scratch, you must be able to display its graphical interface, also referred to as its integrated development environment or IDE. This interface requires that the computer's screen resolution be set to 1024 768 or higher. Anything less and part of the interface will disappear off the screen. Scratch comes packed with all kinds of graphics and audio files that you can use when creating new Scratch projects. As a result, your computer must have at least an extra 120 MB of hard disk space to install Scratch.

Of course, Scratch's minimum hardware requirements are just that, minimum requirements. If your computer's memory and processor exceed the minimum requirements of the operating system, things will run a lot faster and you will be a lot happier. In addition, you will need extra hard drive space beyond the 120 MB minimum required to install Scratch to have a place to store your creations. Scratch lets you create projects that incorporate the use of sound, both as input and output. To take advantage of this feature, your computer will need both speakers and a microphone.

CHAPTER TWO

Scratch Basics

Scratch is a programming language developed to help young people between the ages of 8 and 16 learn 21st-century skills by developing computer programs. The development of Scratch was inspired by the scratching process that DJs use to create new sounds and music by rubbing old-style vinyl records back and forth on record turntables, creating a new and distinctively different sound out of something that already exists. Similarly, Scratch application projects mix graphics and sound to use them in new and different ways. To help get you started with Scratch programming, this chapter provides an overview of the language and reviews the steps that you need to follow to get up and running quickly. The major topics covered in this chapter include: n A review of Scratch's capabilities and uses n Instruction on how to install Scratch on both Microsoft Windows and Mac OS X n A discussion of the benefits of joining Scratch's global community n A demonstration of how to create and execute your first Scratch application project Getting to Know Scratch With a traditional computer and Internet applications, users are limited to working with applications in the way the programmers who developed the applications designed. Scratch turns things around by letting users become programmers. Scratch is designed to meet the needs of young people between 8 and 16, helping to introduce them to computer technology and to improve their learning skills while at the same time facilitating creativity and personal expression. Many people regard computer programming as a mysterious and complex process that requires advanced technical training and education. This is a misperception. Programming languages like BASIC have been around for decades and were developed expressly to teach first-time programmers how to program. In recent years, a new crop of programming languages has appeared, specifically geared toward helping children and students learn to program. One of the very best and newest of these languages is Scratch. Scratch is a visual programming language that is made up of a graphic interface that supports application development in which new projects are created by mixing images, sound, and video under the control of scripts, which specify the application's programming logic. Scripts are created by snapping blocks together, much in the same way that Lego blocks are snapped together to create all sorts of unique creations. Each block represents a different command or action that tells the application how to execute. Scratch also provides programmers with access to all kinds of media, including graphics and sounds as well as tools that can be used to create new graphics and sound files. Scratch is an interpreted programming language. This means that application projects are not precompiled (turned into executable code that can be run as a stand-alone application) before their execution. Instead, the code blocks that makeup Scratch application projects are interpreted and processed each time the application project is executed. Scratch is also a dynamic programming language. It allows changes to be made to application projects even while the projects are executing. As such, Scratch lets programmers experiment by making application changes on the fly to see what type of effect the changes may have on the application's execution.

Imagine—Program—Share!   Scratch's   slogan   is Imagine—Program—Share!

It is designed to encourage teens' creativity by providing them with an easy-to-learn yet powerful programming environment in which they can unleash the power of their imagination. Scratch encourages and facilitates the development of application projects using a mixture of media, graphics, sound, and video to create something new. Scratch provides new programmers with everything needed to create and execute new application projects. Its programming language is designed to make it as easy as possible for new programmers to jump in and get their feet wet and receive immediate feedback on their progress. Scratch promotes an understanding of programming concepts, including conditional and iterative logic, event programming, the use of variables, mathematics, and the use of graphics, and sound effects. By learning to program with Scratch, new programmers develop an understanding and appreciation of the design process, from idea generation to program development, then testing and debugging and the incorporation of user feedback. People, especially kids, love to share, as demonstrated by the amazing success of websites like YouTube, which allows people to share the home video. Sharing is a fundamental part of the Scratch programming experience. Scratch application projects can not only be run on the programmer's desktop but can also be uploaded to the Scratch website, where they can be viewed, executed online, and commented on by other Scratch programmers from around the world. By posting their Scratch application projects on the Scratch website, kids share their experiences and learn from one another and gain gratification and confidence from the experience.

Scratch Uncovered For your convenience, a free trial copy of Scratch (version 1.2.1) is available on this book's companion CD-ROM. In addition, Scratch can be downloaded from the Scratch website located at http://scratch.mit.edu/download. Unlike many programming languages such as Microsoft Visual Basic or C++, Scratch is an open-source project. What this means is that all of the source code that makes up the Scratch programming language is freely available. If you want, you can download a copy of the source code for Scratch at http://scratch.mit.edu/pages/source.

Examples of other open-source programming languages include Ruby and Perl. However, unlike these programming languages developed by a community of programmers working together collectively, Scratch was developed as a closed development project. This means that all Scratch development is performed by the Lifelong Kindergarten Group at MIT Media Lab.

Scratch's Building Block Approach to Programming Scratch is a new programming language, initially released in March 2006. Scratch is different from other programming languages like Visual Basic in that it does not support a text-based approach to programming, as demonstrated here:

```
//Excerpt from a Visual Basic application
If strCurrentAction = "FillCircle" Then
    Dim objCoordinates As Rectangle
        objCoordinates = _
    New Rectangle(Math.Min(objEnd.X, objStart.X), _
    Math.Min(objEnd.Y, objStart.Y), _
    Math.Abs(objEnd.X - objStart.X), _
    Math.Abs(objEnd.Y - objStart.Y))
    Pick_Color_And_Draw("FillCircle", objCoordinates)
End If
```

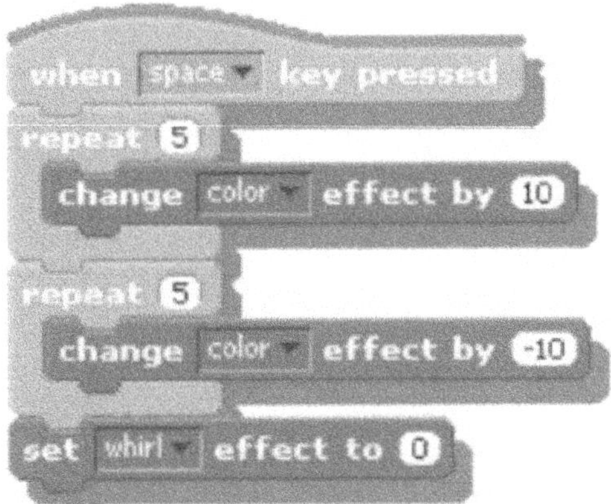

Figure 1.1
An example of how programming logic is outlined in a Scratch application project.

In text-based programming languages, code statements are formulated by following a complex set of syntax rules. Failure to precisely follow these rules when writing statements leads to syntax errors that prevent applications from running. Scratch, on the other hand, uses a different approach. Scratch application projects are built by selecting and snapping together graphical programming blocks, as demonstrated in Figure 1.1. By using code blocks in place of complex program text statements, Scratch significantly simplifies application development while still making use of the same basic programming logic and concepts implemented in other programming languages. As Figure 1.1 demonstrates, each code block represents a different command or action. Blocks fit together like pieces in a puzzle. You can only snap together blocks in ways that make syntactic sense, eliminating syntax errors that proliferate in other programming languages. Some code blocks are configurable, allowing you to specify things like the number of times an action should execute, the text that is to be displayed, or the color to be used when displaying something on the screen. Despite its use of graphical code blocks, Scratch supports the same basic set of programming techniques and constructs as other traditional programming languages. For example, Scratch supports variables, conditional and iterative logic, and event-driven programming. Scratch also supports the manipulation of graphics and the integration of sound into application projects.

Scratch is designed for teaching first-time programmers how to program. To make the learning experience as straightforward and understandable as possible, the developers of Scratch have sometimes sacrificed programming power and features in favor of simplicity and ease of learning. The goal of the Scratch development team is to promote learning and not to develop a programming language capable of delivering every advanced programming feature required by professional programmers. As a result, Scratch lacks some programming features currently supported in advanced programming languages. Instead, Scratch focuses on fundamental programming concepts to provide new programmers with a foundation upon which they can later build, when and if they decide to move on to other programming languages.

Installing Scratch Before you can use Scratch, you need to install it on your computer. The installation process varies, depending on whether you use Microsoft Windows or Mac OS X. Instructions for installing Scratch on both of these operating systems are provided in the sections that follow. You will find the installation files needed to install Scratch 1.2.1 on this book's companion CD-ROM. Alternatively, you can download a copy of Scratch from the Scratch website by executing the following steps: 1. Go to http://scratch.mit.edu and click on the Download Scratch Now! link. 2. The Download Scratch page appears. Fill in the optional form to receive updates about Scratch. 3. Click on the Continue to Scratch Download button. The web page shown in Figure 1.2 displays. Click on the appropriate link for your operating system. The Windows download file is provided as a self-extracting executable named ScratchInstaller.exe. The Mac OS X installation file is provided as a Mac OS X disk image file named MacScratch.dmg. Both of these installation files are approximately 30MB in size, so to download them you will want to use a broadband Internet connection.

Figure 1.2
Downloading either the Mac OS X or Windows version of Scratch.

Installing Java on Windows While Mac OS X comes with Java already installed, Windows does not. Fortunately, installing Java on Microsoft Windows is both free and easy. To do so, go to http://java.com/en/ download as shown in Figure 1.3, and click on the Free Java Download button. Once the online installation process begins, you will need to complete the following steps to finish installing Java: 1. After clicking on the Free Java Download button, you may be prompted by a Windows security window for permission to allow the installation process to continue. If so, click on the Continue button.

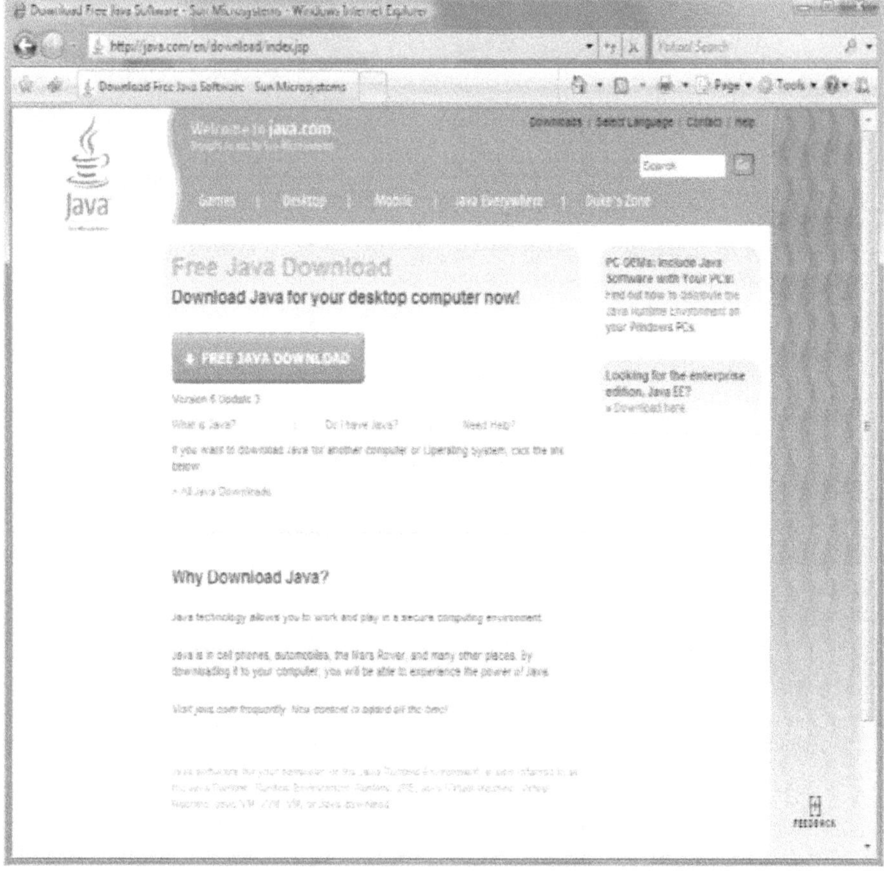

Figure 1.3
Java is required to view and execute Scratch projects loaded onto the Scratch website.

2. Next, a window will appear requesting permission to begin the installation process. Click on the Install button to continue.

3. Finally, a Java Setup Wizard will appear, requiring that you accept the Java License Agreement. Click on the Accept button and then follow the rest of the wizard's instructions to complete the installation process.

Installing Scratch on Windows Scratch installs on Microsoft Windows like any other Windows application. The following procedure outlines the steps involved in completing Scratch's install process:

daddy

1. Double-click on the ScratchInstaller.exe file.

2. If prompted for confirmation, click on Run to allow the installation process to begin.

3. If a security message displays, click on Allow to permit the installation process to continue.

4. The Scratch Setup Wizard will then appear, as demonstrated in Figure 1.4. Click on Next and follow the instructions provided by the wizard to complete the installation process.

5. Once the Scratch Setup Wizard has completed the installation process, you will need to click on the Finish button to close the wizard. Scratch will then automatically start, as demonstrated in Figure 1.5. In addition, a shortcut for Scratch will be added to the Windows desktop.

Figure 1.4
Installing Scratch on Microsoft Windows.

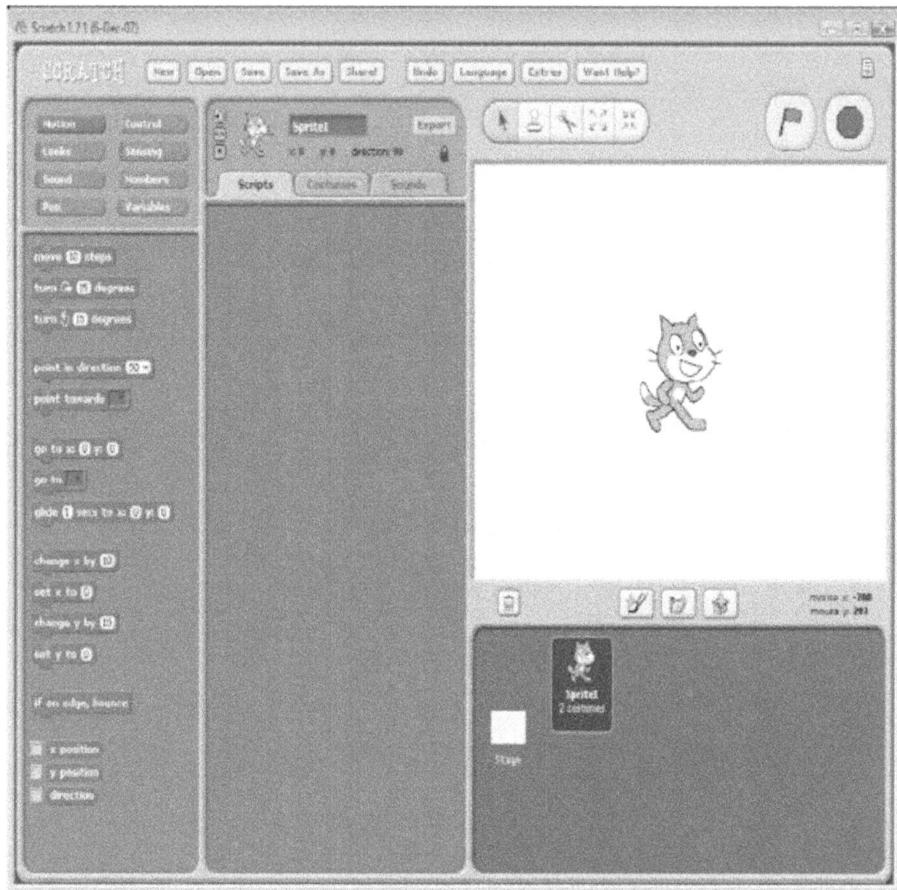

Figure 1.5
Running Scratch on Microsoft Windows Vista.

Installing Scratch on Mac OS X To install Scratch on Mac OS X, double-click on the MacScratch.dmg archive file to open it. Inside you will see a folder named Scratch. Drag and drop the Scratch folder to your Applications folder (or to any other location that you want) to install it. The contents of the Scratch folder are shown in Figure 1.6. To start Scratch and begin working with it, double-click on the Scratch icon, which is represented as a cartoon image of a cat. Within a few moments, the Scratch IDE should appear, as shown in Figure 1.7.

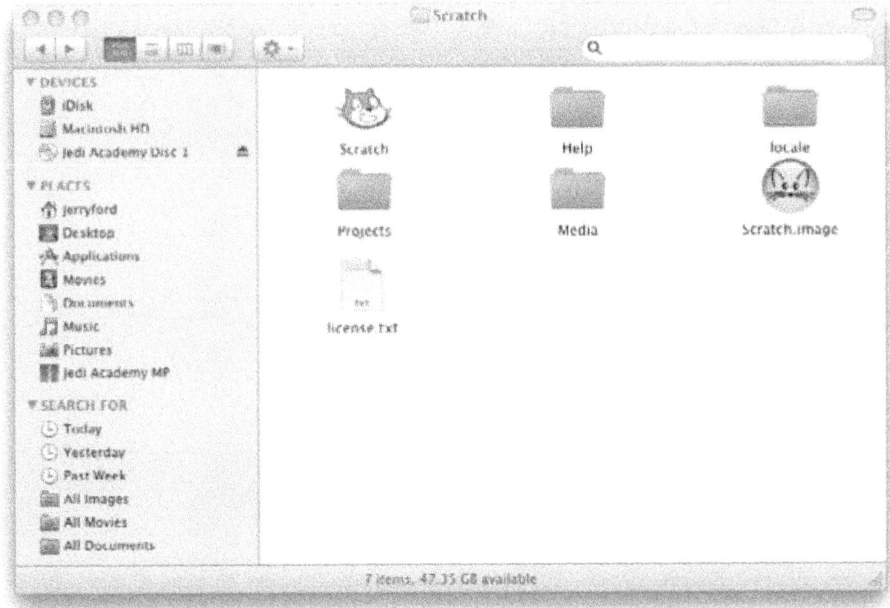

Figure 1.6
Installing Scratch on Mac OS X.

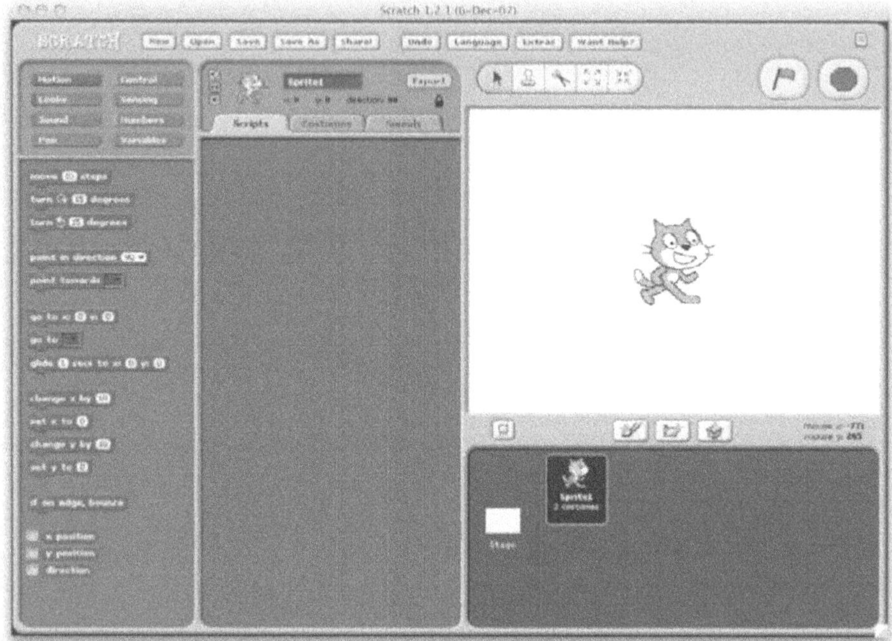

Figure 1.7
Running Scratch on Mac OS X 10.5.

Enter Caption

Creating Your First Scratch Application

Scratch application projects are made up of objects called sprites. A sprite is a two-dimensional bitmap image drawn on a transparent background. Sprites can be moved around and made to interact with one another. Sprites consist of three primary components, as outlined here: n Scripts. Collections of code blocks that outline the programming logic that controls the operation of sprites. n Costumes. Images that are used to display the sprite on an area of the Scratch IDE, referred to as the stage. Sprites can consist of any number of costumes. n Sounds. Sound effects are played during application execution when certain events occur or as background audio. A sprite's appearance can be changed by assigning it different costumes. To move a sprite and control its behavior, you snap together code blocks to create scripts. Sprites can have any number of scripts associated with them. Scripts can be run by double-clicking the code blocks that make them up, in which case each block in the script is executed in top-down order. You can also set things up so that scripts automatically run when various events occur. For example, you can configure script execution to occur when a sprite is clicked or when it interacts with other sprites. Sprites are displayed and interact with one another on a stage. As such, sprites are often referred to as actors. Scratch's stage is located in the upper-right corner of its graphical interface.

Creating a New Scratch Project Now that you are familiar with the basic components of sprites, let's spend a few minutes learning how to create your first Scratch application project. All new Scratch projects automatically contain a single sprite, representing an image of a kitten. By default, the sprite, named Sprite1, does not have any scripts but does have two costumes and two sounds associated with it. Using this sprite, let's create a Scratch application project that makes the kitten meow and say "Hello World!" when clicked. The first step in creating a new Scratch application is to click on the New button located at the top of the Scratch IDE. In response, Scratch will create a new project, as shown in Figure 1.8. As Figure 1.8 shows, the Scratch IDE is organized into several separate components. For starters, the code block area contains code blocks, organized into eight different collections. You will use selected code blocks to create a script that makes the kitten talk.

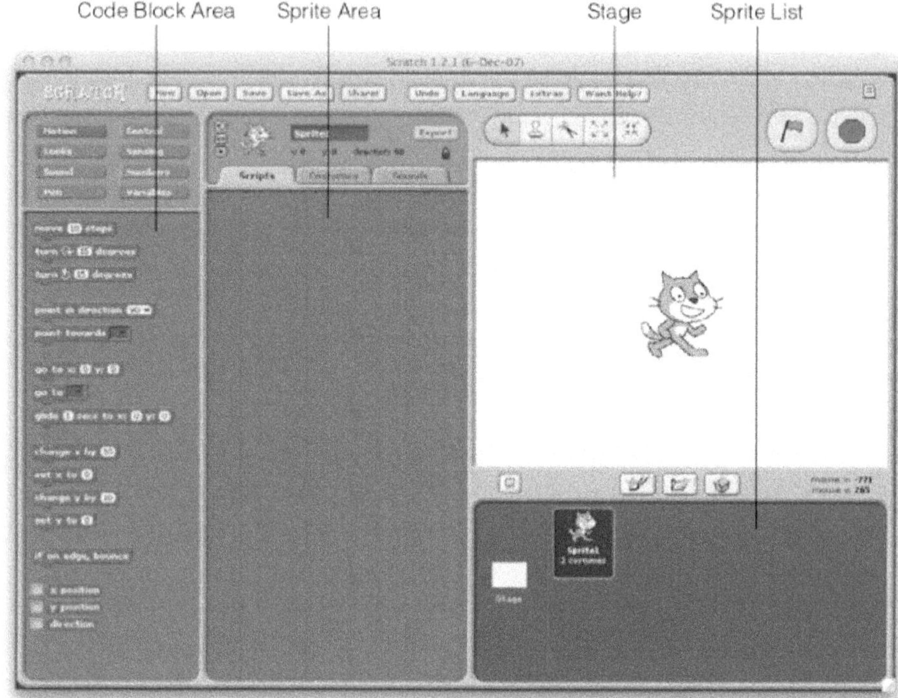

Figure 1.8
Creating a new Scratch application project.

To the right of the code block area is the sprite area. Information about the currently selected sprite is displayed at the top of this area. Just beneath this information are three tabs, which are used to control access to the scripts, costumes, and sounds belonging to the sprite. To the right of the sprite area is the stage, which currently displays the default costume belonging to Sprite1. Just beneath the stage is the sprite list, which displays a list of all the sprites that make up the application project.

Changing Sprite Attributes The application project that you are creating is designed to work with the default sprite. Rather than use the sprite's default name of Sprite1, let's assign it a more descriptive name. To do so, overtype the text displayed at the top of the sprite area with the word Cat. Once you change the name assigned to the sprite, the name change will automatically be reflected in the sprite list. If you look at the entry for the sprite in the sprite list, you should see a picture of the sprite, its new name, and the number of costumes currently assigned to the sprite (you can click on the Costumes tab at the top of the sprite area to view the sprite's costumes). Adding Code Blocks Now that you have changed the name of the sprite, it is time to add the code blocks required to make the cat meow and say "Hello World!" Let's begin by clicking on the Sound button located at the top of the code block area. This displays a collection of code blocks that control the playback of sound effects. Locate the code block labeled play sound and drag and drop it onto the sprite area, as shown in Figure 1.9. By default, this code block is automatically set up to play an audio file that makes a meow sound. Next, click on the Looks button located at the top of the code block area. This displays a collection of code blocks that control the appearance of a sprite. Locate the code block labeled say Hello! for 2 secs and drag and drop it onto the sprite area, as shown in Figure 1.10. By default, this code block displays a text string inside a graphical bubble caption. This code block has two editable fields: a text field and a numeric field. Since the

Figure 1.9
Using a sound block to make the kitten meow.

kitten is supposed to display the message "Hello world!" when clicked, replace the text "Hello!" with "Hello World!". As previously stated, you can run a script at any time by double-clicking on it. To test this, double-click on one of the two code blocks that you have added and then watch the kitten on the stage, and you'll hear it meow and display its message. Rather than having to double-click on the script to make the kitten do its thing, let's set things up so that the kitten automatically meows and talks whenever you click on it. This is accomplished by clicking on the Control button located at the top of the code block area and then dragging and dropping the control block labeled when Cat clicked on top of the two buttons you have already added to the sprite's script, as demonstrated in Figure 1.11. The when Cat clicked block automatically snaps in place as you move it toward the top of the script. With this block now in place, click on the script file and see

Figure 1.10
Using a looks block to make the kitten say something.

what happens. As demonstrated in Figure 1.12, the kitten responds by meowing and talking (displaying "Hello world!" in a text caption bubble). Saving Your Work Okay, now that you have your new Scratch application project working, it is time to save your work. This is done by clicking on the Save button located at the top of the Scratch IDE. In response, the Save

Project window shown in Figure 1.13 displays, allowing you to assign a name to your project and store it on your computer. Type Hello World in the New Filename field to name your application. If you want, you can type your name in the Project Author field and then enter a short description in the About This Project field and then click on the OK button to save your project.

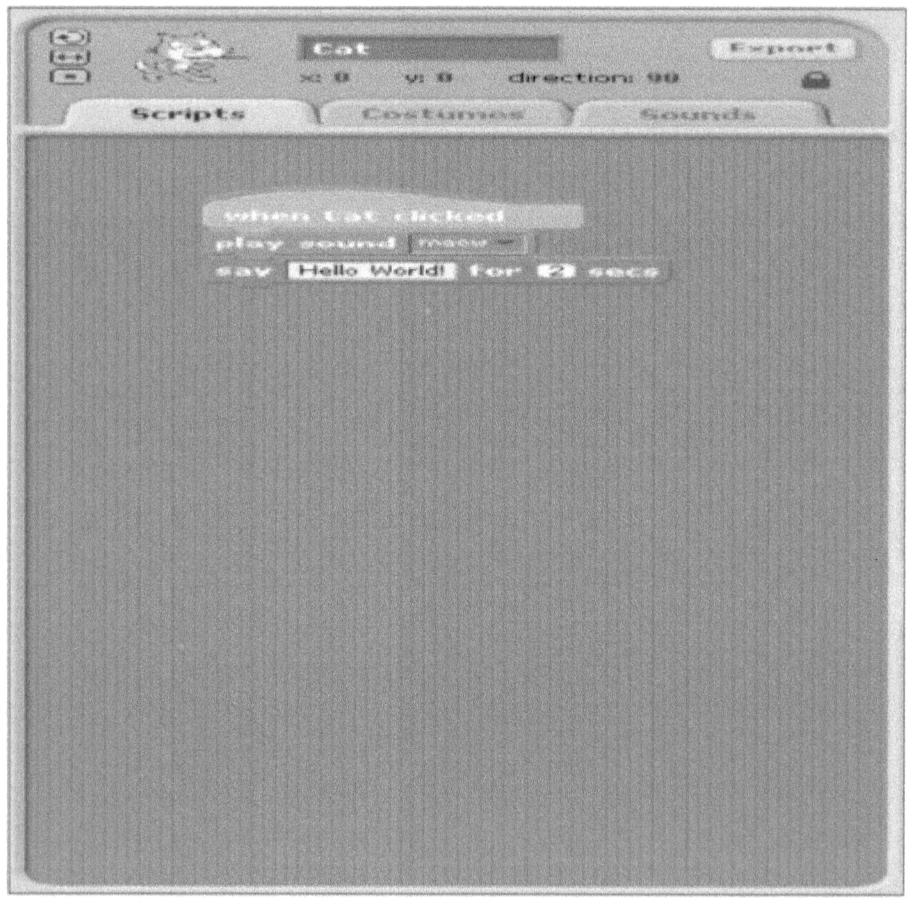

Figure 1.11
Using a control block to control script execution.

That's it. At this point, you have gone through all of the steps necessary to create, test, modify, execute, and then save a new Scratch application project. Now that wasn't too tough, was it? Before wrapping up this chapter, let's spend a few minutes learning about Scratch's global community of users and how you can tap in to learn more about Scratch.

Joining Scratch's Global Community Scratch is supported by a global community of students, teachers, schools, parents, computer enthusiasts, and hobbyists. Scratch is available in many languages, including English, Spanish, German, French, Italian, Hungarian, Hebrew, Polish, Dutch, Romanian, and Russian. The Scratch website is located at http://scratch .mit. Edu as shown in Figure 1.14, helps bring together people from around the world and facilitates the development of the Scratch community.

Figure 1.12
Automating a sprite with a script.

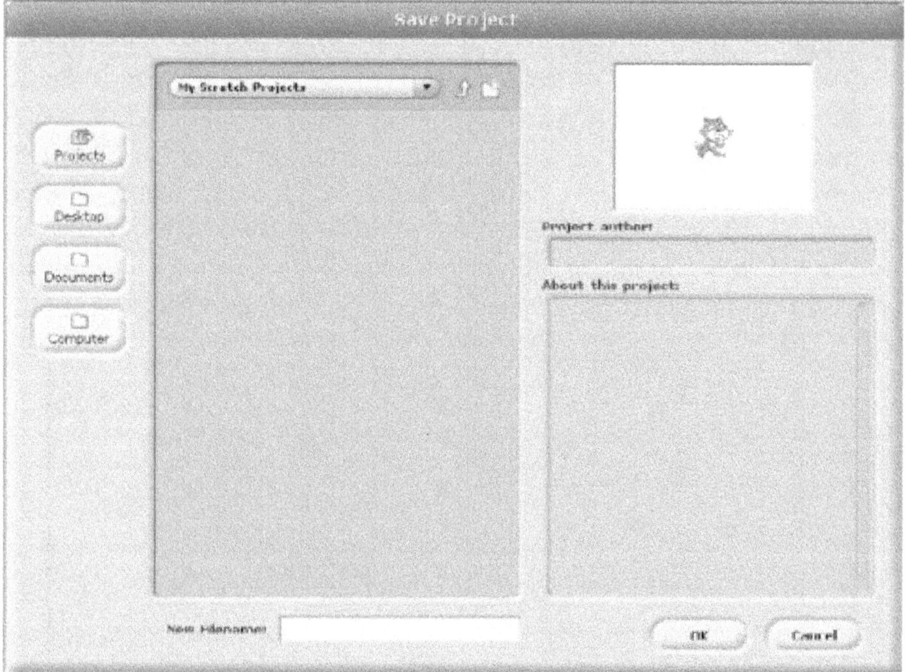

Figure 1.13
Saving your new Scratch application project.

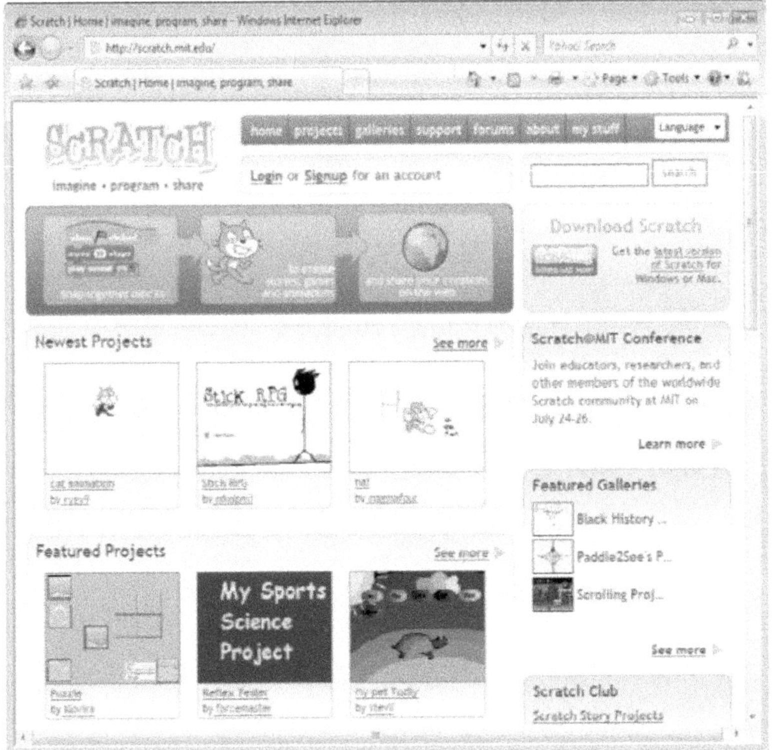

Figure 1.14
The Scratch website is the linchpin supporting the growth and interaction of the Scratch community.

The Scratch website provides access to all kinds of resources that help Scratch programmers learn more about the language. It provides access to online documentation and training videos. It also provides access to the help screen packed with documentation on how to work with Scratch code blocks.

Sharing Your Application Projects The Scratch website promotes application project sharing by allowing Scratch programmers to upload their projects and make them available to anyone visiting the website. This allows Scratch programmers to show off their work and learn from the work of others. Every Scratch project that is uploaded to the website can be downloaded and used as the basis for creating new projects. As

Figure 1.15
The Scratch website facilitates sharing by promoting Scratch projects and making them available for download.

Figure 1.15 shows, the Scratch website actively promotes Scratch applications on its project page (http://scratch.mit.edu/channel/recent), which means that you can expect to see any Scratch projects that you upload posted there as well. The Scratch website lets members post their uploaded Scratch projects in galleries. You can post your Scratch projects in different galleries or create a gallery of your own and even control whether anyone else is allowed to upload their projects into it. As Figure 1.16 demonstrates, the Scratch website actively promotes member galleries.

Figure 1.16
You can create your own gallery and use it to promote your programming skills.

If you decide to create your gallery, you can customize it by assigning it a name and a description and by determining whether you want to let anyone else upload Scratch projects into it.

Registering with the Scratch Website To upload your Scratch projects to the Scratch website, you must sign up for a free account, which you can do by clicking on the signup link at the top of every page on the Scratch website. Clicking on this link opens the Create an Account page, shown in Figure 1.17. The Scratch website gives its members the ability to comment on any Scratch application project that is uploaded to the website. The

website also provides

Figure 1.17
Registering for a free account on the Scratch website.

access to a collection of forums designed to host a conversation between students, teachers, and Scratch enthusiasts from all over the world.

Summary

This chapter has provided an overview of the Scratch language and its capabilities. It showed you how to install Scratch on your computer and then demonstrated how to create your first Scratch application. It also introduced you to the Scratch website and explained the importance of setting up an account and becoming an active member of the Scratch community.

CHAPTER THREE

The Scratch Development Environment

To become an effective Scratch programmer, you need to become intimately familiar with its integrated development environment, or IDE. In this chapter, you will learn about the stage at which applications execute and the sprite list that Scratch uses to display and organize sprites used in your applications. You will also learn how to work with editors that create scripts, costumes, and sound effects. You will also learn all about Scratch's paint program, which you can use to create your custom graphics files. By the time you have completed this chapter, you will have a solid understanding of all of the features and capabilities of the Scratch IDE and will be ready to begin using it to create your Scratch application projects.

Getting Comfortable with the Scratch IDE Scratch is a graphical programming language. Scratch applications are created by executing Scratch projects made up of different types of media, including graphics and sound, using scripts made up of different code blocks. Scratch projects are created using its IDE. As shown in Figure 2.1, Scratch's IDE is composed of numerous components.

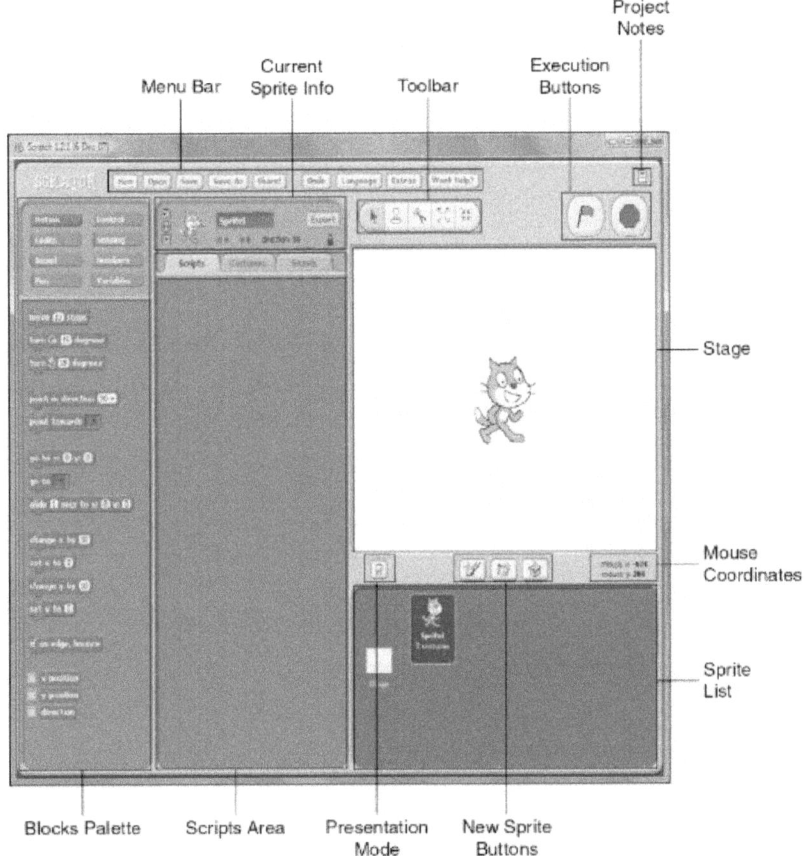

Figure 2.1
The Scratch IDE facilitates the development and execution of Scratch applications.

Together, all of the components identified in Figure 2.1 provide a robust and powerful, yet initiative and fun, work environment, providing everything needed to develop Scratch applications. The rest of this chapter will offer a detailed overview of each of the major components that make up the Scratch IDE. Getting Familiar with Menu Bar Commands

Like most graphic applications, the Scratch IDE has a menu bar made up of a collection of buttons located at the top of the IDE, as shown in Figure 2.2. These buttons provide access to commands that allow you to create, open, and save Scratch projects as well as share them on the Internet, undo previous commands, change the language used by the IDE, and much more.

The following list explains each of the buttons that make up the menu bar.

n New. Creates a new Scratch application project. n Open. Opens an existing Scratch application project.

n Save. Saves the current Scratch project (with a file extension of .sb).

n Save As. Saves the current Scratch project under a new name.

n Share! Uploads a copy of the project to the Scratch website (http://scratch .mit. Edu) where it can be made available for viewing and downloaded by other Scratch programmers.

n Undo. Restores the last script, code block, or sprite deleted from the application project during the current working session.

n Language. Lets you specify the language to be used by the Scratch IDE. n Extras. Displays a popup list from which you can select one of the following commands: Import Project, Start Single Stepping, Compress Sounds, or Compress Images.

Figure 2.2
The menu bar provides easy access to commands that you can use to create and save Scratch projects.

Want Help? Displays a page that provides a link to the Scratch website as well as to the following set of resources: Reference Materials, Tutorials, or Frequently Asked Questions.

Most of the commands listed above are self-explanatory. However, the last three commands merit additional explanation. When clicked, the Language button displays a menu of programming languages from which you can select. Depending on the language selected, a complete translation may be available. In other cases, only scripts and code blocks may be translated.

When clicked, the Extras button displays a menu that has the following options. n About. Displays a popup window that provides information about the version of Scratch being used. n Import Project. This command imports all of the sprites and backgrounds, along with any related scripts, from the specified project into the current project. As such, this command makes the sharing and movement of sprites and backgrounds between Scratch project a snap. n Start Single Stepping. This command tells Scratch to execute an application a step at a time, allowing you to observe the execution flow of code blocks. This command will be discussed more thoroughly in Chapter 15, "Finding and Fixing Program Errors." n Compress Sounds. This command compresses any sound files used by the current application project to reduce the project's size. This is important because the Scratch website imposes a 10MB limit on the size of Scratch applications. n Compress Images. Like the Compress Sounds command, this command compresses any graphic image files used by the current application project to reduce the project's size. By compressing the size of your application, you can sometimes reduce large Scratch projects enough to allow them to upload. 30 Chapter 2 n Getting Comfortable The last button on Scratch's menu bar is the Want Help? button. When clicked, this button opens a browser window that provides access to the following resources. n Getting Started. Opens the "Getting Started with Scratch" PDF user guide. n Help Screens. Displays a collection of help screens that document the use and purpose of every Scratch code block. n Reference Guide. Opens the Scratch "Reference Guide" PDF reference file. n, Visit the Scratch support page. Displays the Scratch support web page located at http://scratch.wik.is/ Support.

Running Scratch Applications on the Stage The stage is the area on the Scratch IDE, located on the upper-right side, where your Scratch applications execute. The stage provides a place for the sprites that make up your applications to interact with one another and the user.

The stage is 480 units wide and 360 units high. The stage is mapped out into a logical grid using a coordinate system made up of an X-axis and a Y-axis, as demonstrated in. As you can see, the X-axis runs from coordinates 240 to −240, and the Y-axis coordinate runs from coordinates 180 to −180. The middle of the stage has a coordinate location of (0, 0). Scratch keeps you informed of the pointer's location whenever it is moved over the stage by displaying its (X, Y) coordinate position in the mouse x: and mouse y: fields just beneath the bottom-right side of the stage. The stage can be assigned one or more backgrounds, allowing you to change its appearance during application execution. By default, all Scratch applications are assigned a blank background. You can add new backgrounds by clicking on the Stage thumbnail, located on the left-hand side of the sprite list, and then clicking on the Backgrounds tab located just above the scripts area. Like sprites, the stage can be assigned its scripts and sound effects. Tip If you right-click on an open area on the stage, a popup menu will appear, displaying the following menu items: n Grab screen region for the new sprite. Makes a copy of a selected portion of the stage and uses it to create a new sprite. n, Save a picture of the stage. Saves a copy of the stage as a . GIF file.

Running Applications in Presentation Mode As you saw in Chapter 1 when you created the Hello World project, Scratch runs your applications on the stage within the IDE by default. However, if you click on the Presentation Mode button, located just beneath the bottom-left corner of the stage, you can run your Scratch application project in Presentation mode. To see how this works, click on the Open button located at the top of the Scratch IDE and then locate and open the Hello World project. Next, click on the Presentation Mode button to switch to full-screen mode. Once in Presentation screen mode, single-click on the sprite representing the kitten and watch as your application executes, as demonstrated in Figure 2.5. You can exit Presentation mode at any time either by clicking on the Exit Presentation Mode icon located just above the upper-left side of the stage or by pressing the Escape key. Controlling Application Execution Whether running your application from the IDE's stage or in Presentation mode, you can automatically start any scripts that begin with the green flag control block by clicking on the green flag button located in the upper-right corner of the IDE, as shown in Figure 2.6. This same button is also available in Presentation mode. By clicking on the red stop button located right next to the green flag

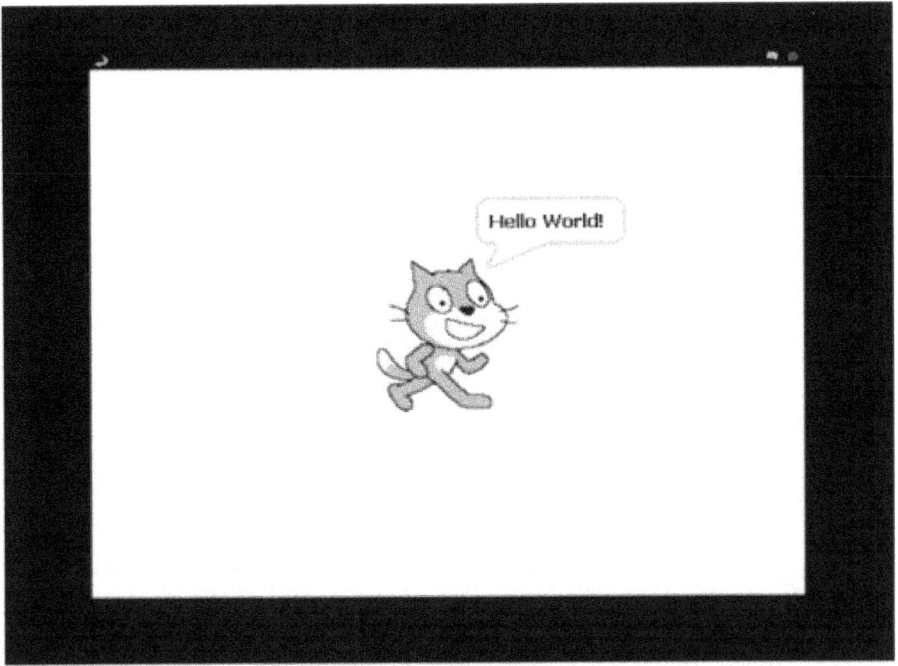

Figure 2.5
Running a Scratch application project in Presentation mode.

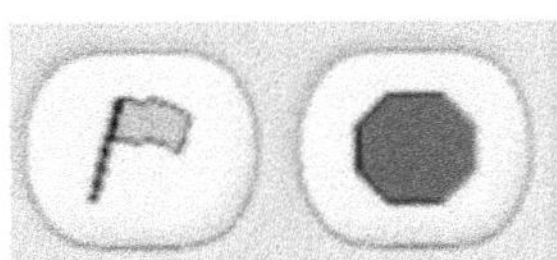

Figure 2.6
The green flag and red stop buttons provide control over script execution.

button, you can stop the execution of your applications any time you finish working with them.

Working with the Sprite List Scratch applications are made up of sprites that interact with one another as they move around the stage. Each sprite that makes up a Scratch application is displayed as a thumbnail in the sprite list area, located on the lower-right portion of the Scratch IDE, as shown in Figure 2.7. Although it has no impact on a Scratch application, you can reorganize the order in which sprites are displayed in the sprite list by dragging and dropping thumbnails to any location that makes sense to you. In addition to a thumbnail, Scratch also displays the name of each sprite as well as the number of scripts and costumes belonging to each sprite. To work with a sprite and edit its scripts, costumes, and sound effects, just click on its thumbnail. The currently selected sprite is highlighted by a blue outline. Once selected, you can click on the Scripts, Costumes, and Sounds tabs located at the top of the script area to edit a sprite's scripts, costumes, and sound effects.

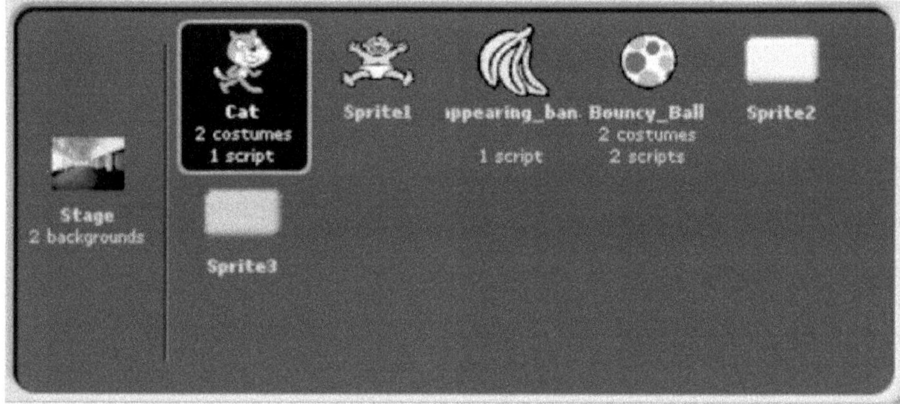

Figure 2.7
The sprite list displays a thumbnail for each sprite in an application.

If you right-click on a sprite's thumbnail, the following list of menu options is displayed: n Show. Centers a sprite on the stage, placing it on top of all other sprites. n Export this sprite. Exports a sprite as a file, making it available to be imported into other Scratch projects. n Duplicate. Makes a copy of the sprite. n Delete. Removes a sprite from the project.

The sprite list also displays a thumbnail representing the application project's stage. When the stage's thumbnail is selected, you can add scripts to the stage, modify the stage's background by assigning it one or more graphic files, and also add sounds to the stage.

Generating New Sprites Scratch makes it easy for you to work with sprites by providing three different options for adding them to your applications. These options are accessed through the New Sprite buttons located just below the stage, as shown in Figure 2.8. When clicked, the Paint New Sprite button starts Scratch's Paint Editor program. This program provides everything you need to draw new sprites on a transparent

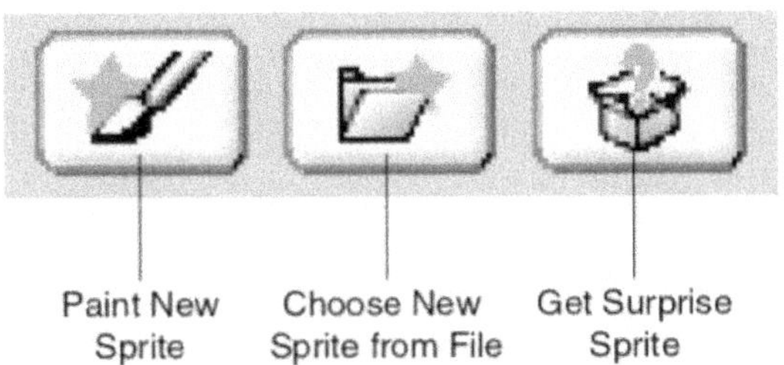

Figure 2.8
The New Sprite buttons provide access to tools for adding and creating new sprites.

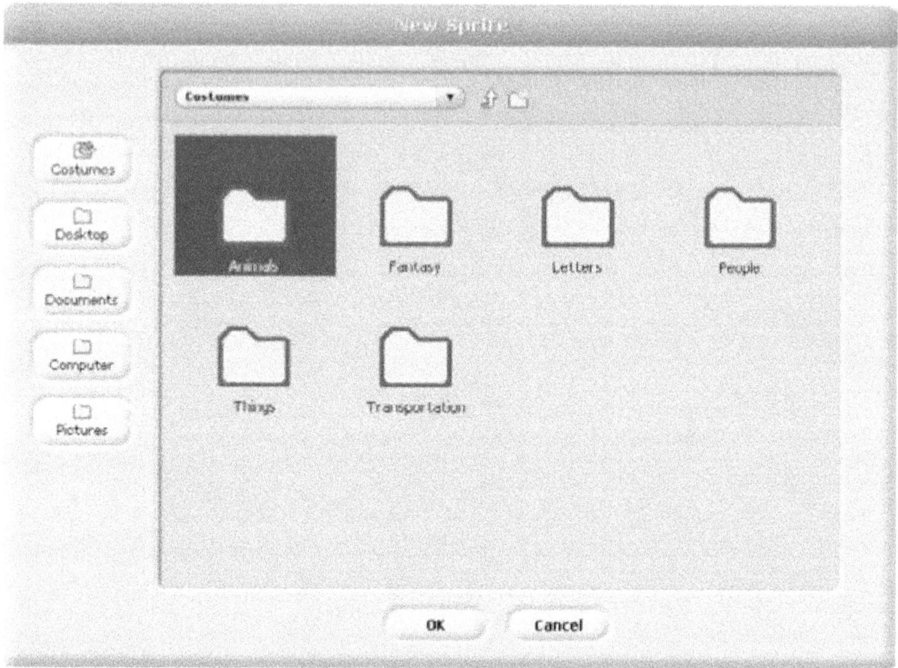

Figure 2.9
Scratch supplies easy access to a wide selection of ready-made sprites.

background. You will learn the ins and outs of how to work with the Paint Editor program a little later in this chapter. When clicked, the Choose New Sprite from File button displays the New Sprite window shown in Figure 2.9, providing access to different collections of graphic files that you can add to your Scratch applications as sprites. To select and add a sprite, all you have to do is to drill down into one of Scratch's folders, find the sprite you want, and then click on the OK button. The sprite that you selected will then appear in the center of the stage, and a thumbnail representing the sprite will be added to the sprite list. The Get Surprise Sprite button randomly retrieves one of Scratch's ready-made sprites and adds it to your application project. It can be used to generate all kinds of wacky projects.

Tracking Mouse Pointer Location As you learn how to develop your Scratch applications, you will need to keep track of the initial placement and subsequent movement of sprites on the stage. Scratch assists you in this task by keeping track of mouse-pointer movement whenever you move the pointer across the stage (see Figure 2.10). You can use

Figure 2.10
The Scratch IDE makes it easy to track the mouse-pointer's location when it moves around the stage.

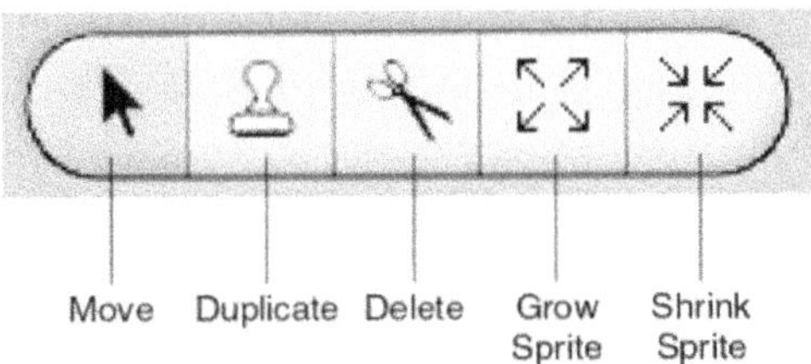

Figure 2.11
The Scratch toolbar provides tools for interacting with sprites.

this information identifies the coordinates data that you need to incorporate into your application code as you develop the programming logic that drives your Scratch projects.

Working with the Scratch Toolbar Another important component of the Scratch IDE is the toolbar, shown in Figure Figure 2.11. The toolbar provides access to commands that you can use to interact with and control the sprites that make up your applications. The following list summarizes the functionality provided by each of the toolbar's buttons: n Move. Allows you to drag and drop sprites to different locations on the stage (default toolbar selection). n Duplicate. Makes a copy of the currently selected sprite, including its scripts, costumes, and sounds, providing an easy way of adding new sprites to your applications. Once a sprite is duplicated, you can customize the new copy of the sprite as you see fit. n Delete. Removes a sprite, including all its scripts, costumes, and sounds, from the project and removes its thumbnail from the sprite list.

n Grow Sprite. Increases a sprite's size, in case its actual size does not meet the needs of your application. n Shrink Sprite. Decreases a sprite's size, in case its actual size does not meet the needs of your application. By default, the Move button is always selected. However, you may select any of the other toolbar buttons by clicking on them and then clicking on the sprite that you want to work with.

Switching Between Code Block Groups Like applications created by any programming language, Scratch applications execute program code made up of collections of code blocks that manipulate sprites and interact with the user. Scratch's program code is organized into scripts belonging to sprites. Every sprite in an application can be assigned one or more scripts. In addition, the stage can also execute its scripts. As you have already seen, the first step in creating a script is to select the sprite (or the stage) to which the script will belong. This is done by clicking on the appropriate thumbnail in the sprites list. You can then add code blocks by dragging the blocks from the blocks palette and dropping them into the scripts area (when the Script tab is selected). The block palette is organized into two sections. The top section contains eight-button controls, each of which represents a different category of a code block. Each of the buttons is color coded. The currently selected button is easily identified because it is filled in with its assigned color. The left-hand edge of the unselected buttons shows the color of the code blocks belonging to their category. For example, Figure 2.12 shows how the block palette looks when the Motion button has been selected.

Getting Comfortable with the Scripts Area The last major part of the Scratch IDE that you need to become familiar with is the scripts area, which consists of two major sections. The Current Sprite Info section, located at the top of the scripts area, displays information about the currently selected sprite. The rest of the script area is controlled by three tabs, which allow you to add scripts, costumes, and sounds to sprites.

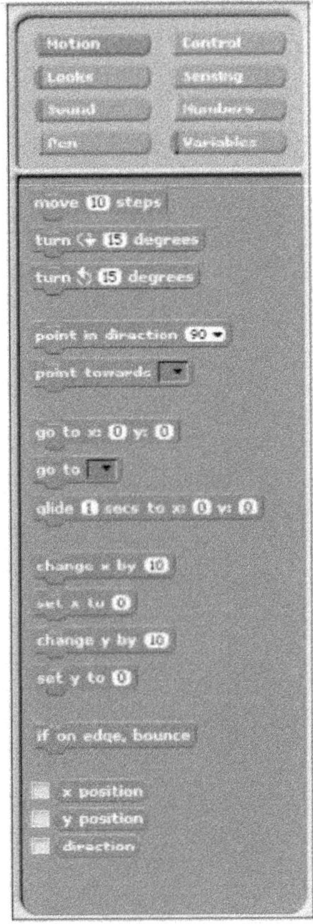

Figure 2.12
Each category of code block is designed to accomplish a related set of tasks.

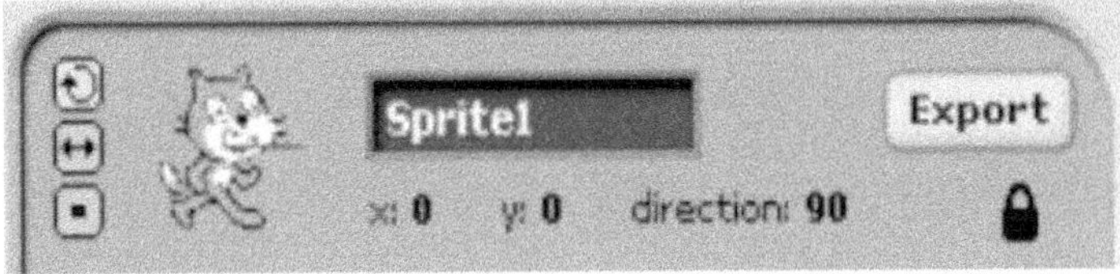

Figure 2.13
Changing a sprite's name and viewing detailed information about the sprite.

Examining Sprite Details The Current Sprite Info section displays the name currently assigned to the selected sprite, which, as demonstrated in Figure 2.13, is Sprite1. You can change a sprite's name by typing over it. The sprite's current coordinates and direction are displayed just beneath its name, and the sprite's currently assigned costume is displayed just to the left of its name.

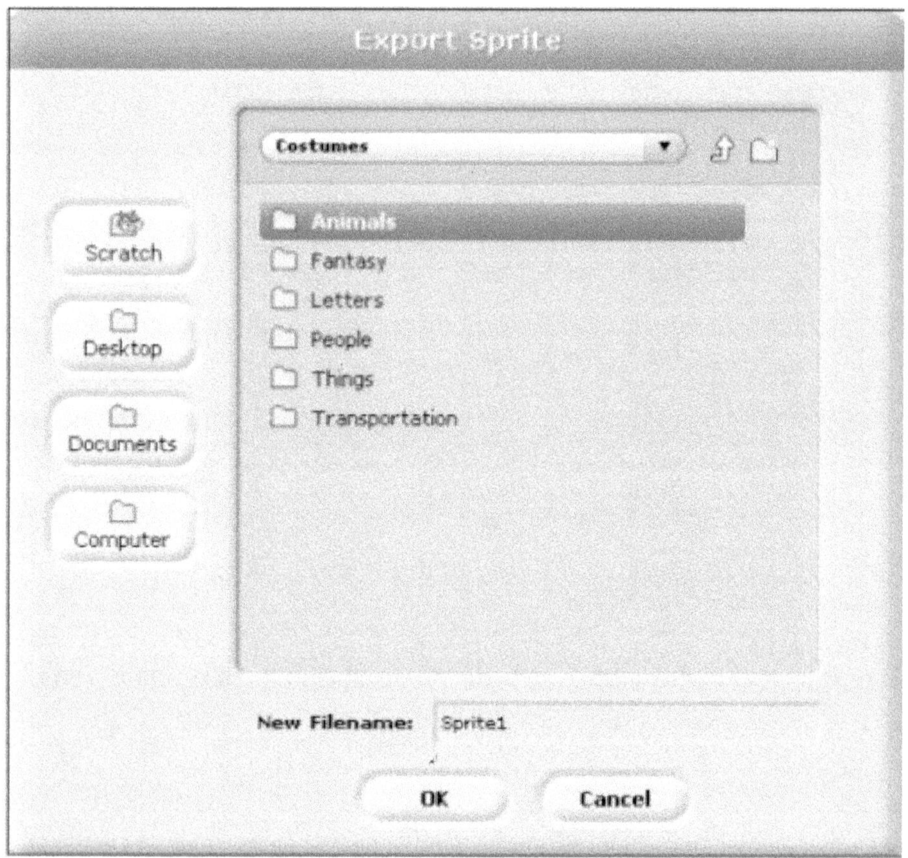

Figure 2.14
Exporting a sprite as a stand-alone graphic file.

Take note of the blue line that is displayed on the thumbnail in the Current Sprite Info section. It shows the sprite's currently assigned direction. You can change the sprite's direction by dragging the outside edge of this line in a new direction. If you do not like the direction that you have set for the sprite, double-click on the sprite to reset it back to its default direction (90-degree angle). You can export the scripts as a stand-alone line by clicking on the Export button. This opens the Export Sprite window shown in Figure 2.14, allowing you to specify the location where you want to save the sprite, making it available for use in other Scratch application projects. Just beneath the Export button is a graphic file representing a padlock. Clicking on this image toggles the graphic between a locked and unlocked state. When set to locked, Scratch prevents the sprite from being dragged around the stage by the user when the script is run in Presentation mode or when run from the Scratch website. Just to the left of the sprite's currently selected costume are three buttons that you can use to specify the sprite's rotation style. These three buttons are mutually exclusive, meaning that you can only select one. Table 2.1 identifies the rotational style represented by each of these buttons.

Table 2.1 Sprite Rotational Buttons

Button	Name	Description
	Can rotate	Rotates the sprite's costume by 360 degree when the sprite's direction is changed.
	Only face left-right	Toggles the direction that the sprite's costume faces from left to right and vice versa.
	Don't rotate	Maintains the sprite costume's current direction.

Editing Scripts As you have already seen, Scratch scripts are created by dragging code blocks from the blocks palette onto the scripts area (when the Scripts tab has been selected). Of course, the code blocks must be added in a manner that makes logical sense, which is what Chapters 5 through 22 are designed to teach you.

Adding Costumes A sprite can have one or more costumes, allowing it to change its appearance as an application executes. A sprite must have at least one costume. For example, Figure 2.15 shows a sprite that has two costumes. Each costume is assigned a unique name and number (displayed just to the left of the costume's image). By default, Scratch only displays a sprite's first costume. You can drag and drop costumes to change their position in the list. When moved, the number assigned to the costume is automatically changed as well. Scratch gives you three different ways of adding new costumes to sprites. For starters, you can click on the Paint button. This opens the Paint Editor program,

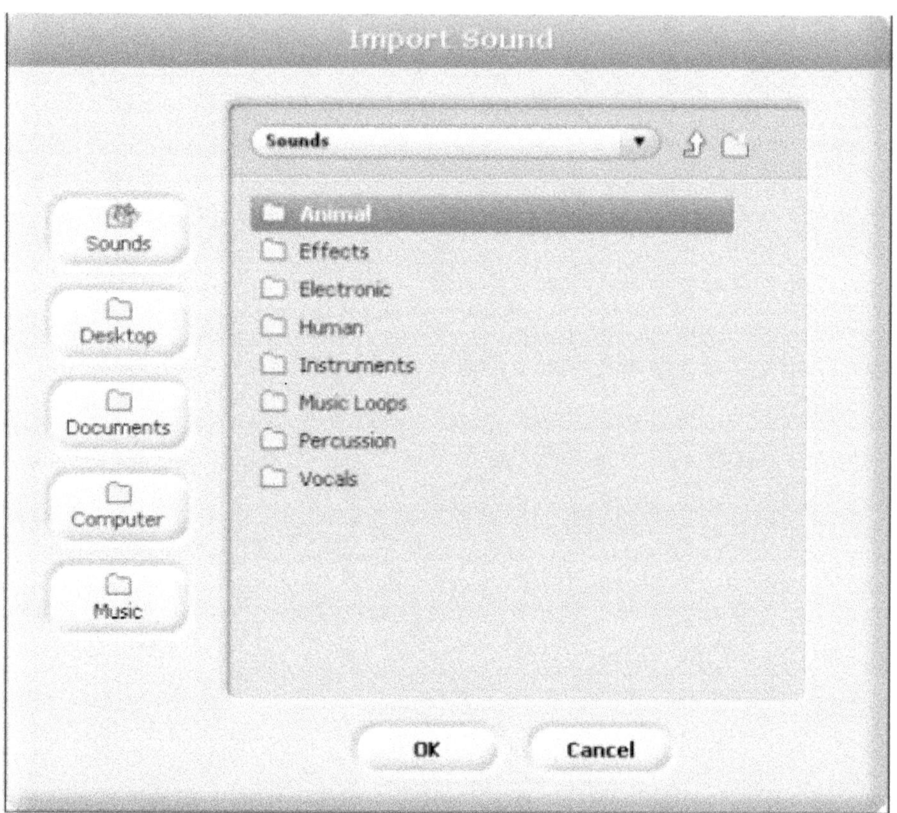

Figure 2.15
Importing and assigning a sound file to a sprite.

which you can use to draw a new costume. You can also add a new costume to a sprite by clicking on the Import button and specifying an image file from a folder on your computer. Lastly, you can drag and drop an image file from the Internet or your desktop onto the scripts area when the Costumes tab is selected.

Once added, you can modify a costume by selecting it and clicking on the Edit button, which opens the Paint Editor. You can also add a new costume to a sprite by selecting an existing costume and then clicking on the Copy button. Once the copy of the costume has been added, you can click on its Edit button, allowing you to modify it using the Paint Editor. You can delete a costume from a sprite by selecting it and then clicking on the round Delete button to the right of the Copy button. You can also turn a costume into a sprite or export it as a stand-alone costume by right-clicking on it and selecting the appropriate option from the popup menu that appears. 42 Chapter 2 n Getting Comfortable Figure 2.15 Importing and assigning a sound file to a sprite. Note The stage can be assigned a graphic to be used as a background upon which the application's sprites are displayed. The stage can be assigned a series of backgrounds, allowing an application to change backgrounds during application execution. To view, edit, and make a copy of a background, select the stage thumbnail located in the sprite list. When you do this, the Costumes tab in the scripts area changes to the Backgrounds tab, allowing you to modify and work with application backgrounds. From here you can also create new backgrounds yourself by clicking on the Paint button. This opens Scratch's Paint Editor program, discussed later in this chapter, allowing you to create any background you want. You can also click on the Import button to add an external graphic file to your application as a background.

Adding Sound Effects Just as sprites can have different costumes, you can also assign one or more sounds to them (or to the stage), which can be played during application execution, either as background music or noise or as sound effects during gameplay. Scratch can play back MP3 files as well as most WAV, AU, and AIF audio files. To view the sound files associated with a sprite or to record or import a new file, select the sprite's thumbnail in the sprite list and then click on the Sounds tab in the scripts area. A list of the sound files belonging to the sprite is displayed, as demonstrated in Figure 2.16.

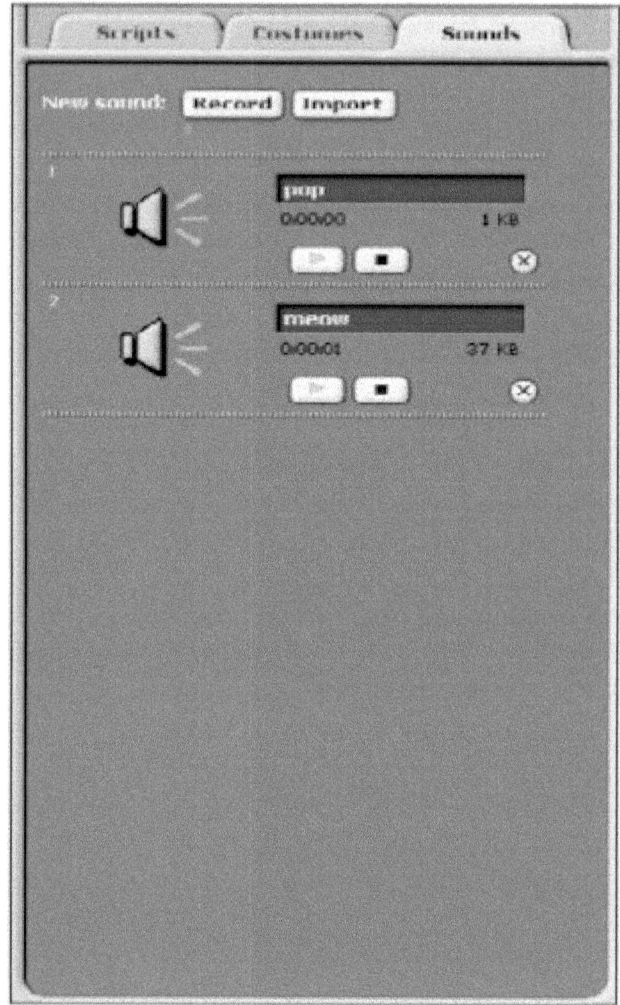

Figure 2.16
Adding and editing sound files.

Once the Sounds tab has been selected, you can perform any of the following actions on any sound files that belong to the sprite: n Change the name used to refer to the sound within the application. n, Click on the Play button to listen to the sound. n Click on the Stop button to halt sound playback. n, Click on the Delete button to remove the sound from the application project. In addition to interacting with a sprite's existing sound file, you may add new sound files by clicking on the Record button. In response, the Sound Recorder window appears, as shown in Figure 2.17, allowing you to record and save a new sound file. Of course, to record your sound files, your computer will need to have a microphone. You can also add new sound files to your Scratch application by clicking on the Import button, which opens the Import Sound window, as shown in Figure 2.18, allowing you to select a sound file. Scratch provides access to tons of prerecorded sound files. By default, the Import Sound window displays a listing of folders containing different collections of sound files. Keeping Project Notes Another important feature of the Scratch IDE is the ability to add and update project notes. Scratch allows you to add project notes when you first save your application project. Once they are saved, you may update your project's notes at any time by clicking on the Project Notes icon located in the upper-right corner of the IDE. In response, the Project Notes window displays, as demonstrated in Figure 2.19.

Figure 2.17
Recording a new audio file to be used as part of a Scratch application.

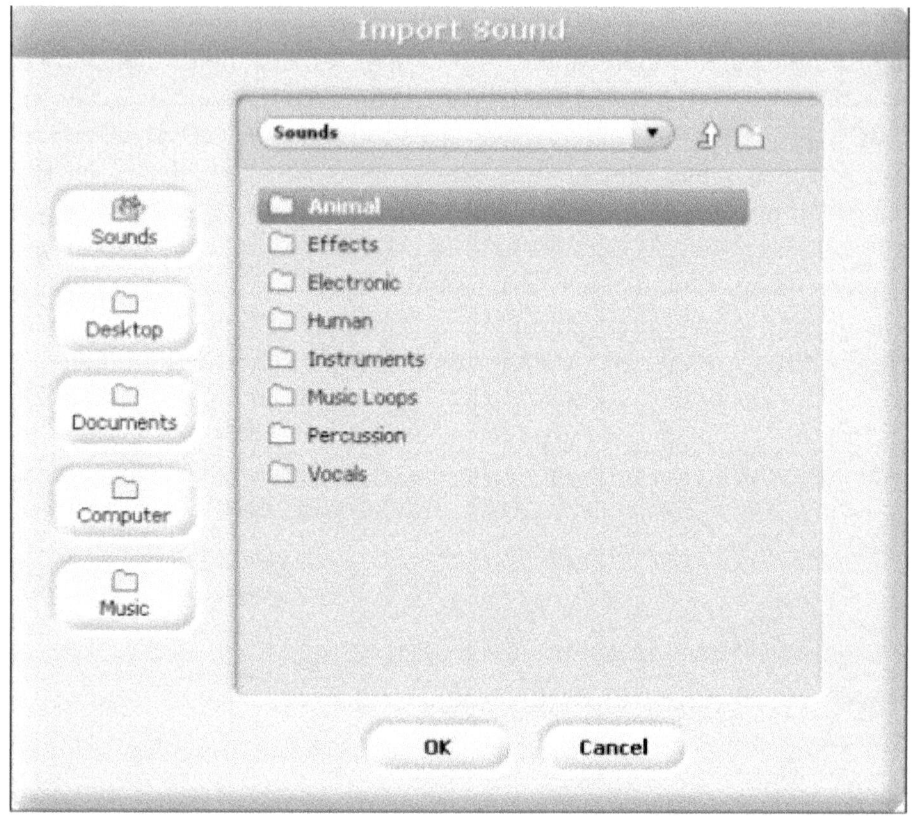

Figure 2.18
Importing and assigning a sound file to a sprite.

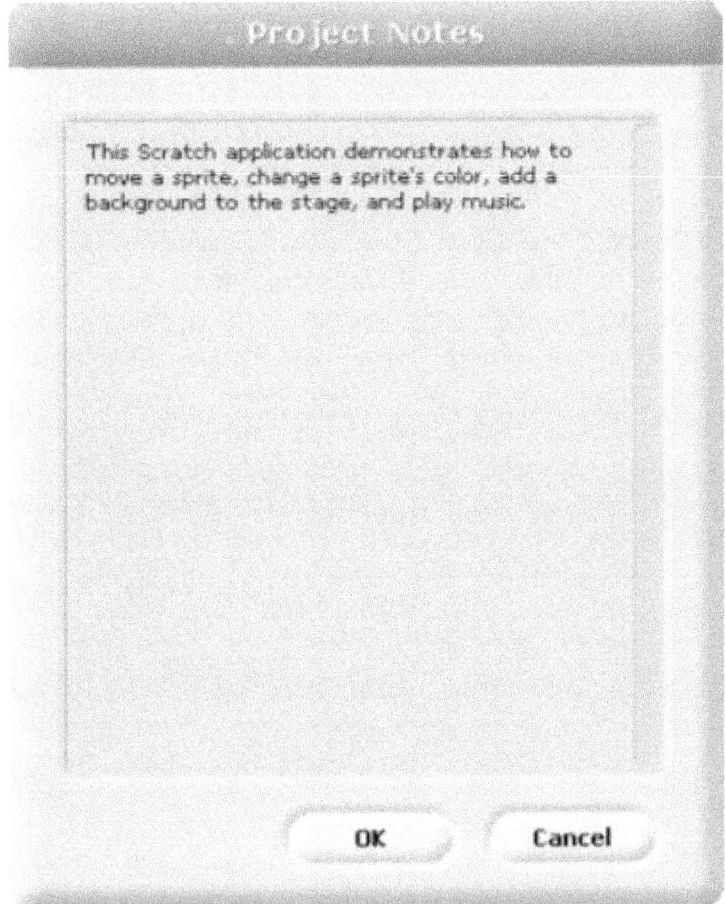

Figure 2.19
Viewing and updating Scratch application project notes.

The Project Notes window operates like a simple Notepad program, allowing you to type in any text you want.

Creating New Sprites Using Scratch's Paint Editor In addition to using the sprites supplied with Scratch and graphics that you acquire from the Internet, you can always create your sprite using any graphic/paint program. Although it does not have all of the bells and whistles that applications like Corel Paint Shop Pro or Adobe Photoshop have, Scratch's built-in Paint Editor, shown in Figure 2.20, offers everything needed to draw or modify graphics for use as sprites and backgrounds. As Figure 2.20 demonstrates, Scratch's Paint Editor is divided into multiple components. Thanks to Scratch's cross-platform design, the Paint Editor looks and operates identically on both Microsoft Windows and Mac OS X. Examining the Drawing Canvas Links to the Paint Editor program are located just under the stage and within the Costumes and Backgrounds tabs located in the scripts area. The Paint Editor program can be used to create or modify new sprites, costumes, and backgrounds. Most of the space on the Paint Editor's window is dedicated to a drawing canvas. To draw on the canvas, you select different drawing commands from the toolbar and then use the mouse to draw on the canvas. You can work with different colors and apply a range of special effects. If the size of the graphic being worked on exceeds the available area, scrollbars are enabled on the right-hand side and the bottom of the drawing canvas, allowing you to view all parts of the graphic. You can also use the Zoom In and Zoom Out buttons located at the bottom of the Paint Editor window to temporarily increase or decrease the magnification of the drawing canvas.

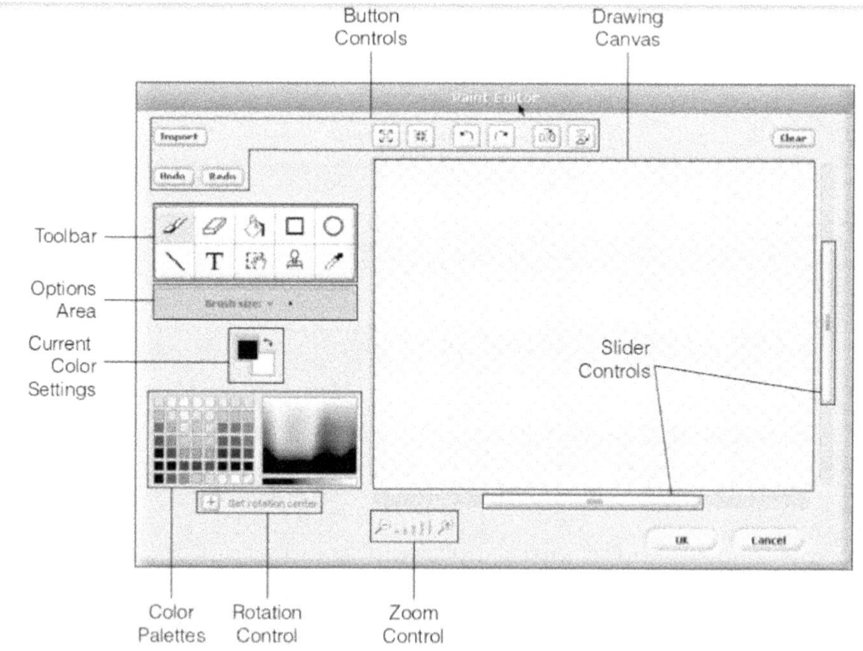

Figure 2.20
Scratch's built-in Paint Editor program provides everything needed to create sprites and costumes.

Working with the Toolbar and Options Area When creating or editing a graphic image on the drawing canvas, the buttons located on the Paint Editor's toolbar provide access to essential features and functionality. The following list offers an overview of the functionality provided by each toolbar button: n Paintbrush. Allows you to draw freehand on the drawing canvas using the current foreground color and brush size. n Eraser. Allows you to erase selected portions of the drawing canvas using the current eraser size. Erased portions of the drawing canvas are returned to a transparent state. Creating New Sprites Using Scratch's Paint Editor 47 Slider Controls Drawing Canvas Button Controls Rotation Control Color Palettes Options Area Toolbar Current Color Settings Zoom Control Figure 2.20 Scratch's built-in Paint Editor program provides everything needed to create sprites and costumes. n Fill. Allows you to fill in enclosed areas with either a gradient or a solid color, depending on the selected option specified in the options area. n Rectangle. Allows you to draw filled-in or outlined rectangle shapes using the current foreground color. n Ellipse. Allows you to draw filled-in or outlined ellipses using the current foreground color. n Line. Allows you to draw straight lines using the current foreground color. n Text. Allows you to include text as part of a drawing using the current font type and size. n Selection. Allows you to select a rectangular portion of the drawing canvas and move it to a different part of the drawing canvas (cut and paste). n Stamp. Allows you to select a rectangular portion of the drawing canvas and copy it to different parts of the drawing canvas (copy and paste). n Eyedropper. Allows you to select the foreground color. Most of the toolbar buttons accept configuration options that further refine the functionality provided by the button control. For example, Figure 2.21 shows the four configuration options that are provided when the Fill button has been selected. These options set the fill style that is applied and includes the application of a solid color and the use of a horizontal gradient, vertical gradient, or radial gradient. Note A gradient is a color created by blending the foreground and background colors.

Figure 2.21
The content of the options area changes based on the selected toolbar button.

Working with Button Controls As shown in Figure 2.22, Scratch's Paint Editor program includes several button controls that can initiate an assortment of different actions. The following list identifies each of these buttons and explains its purpose: n Import. Opens an image from a graphic file stored on your computer. n Grow. Increases the size of the drawing canvas, allowing you to focus on a particular area. n Shrink. Decreases the size of the drawing canvas. n Rotate counterclockwise. Rotates the drawing canvas counterclockwise. n Rotate clockwise. Rotates the Drawing canvas clockwise. n Flip horizontally. Flips the drawing canvas horizontally. n Flip vertically. Flips the drawing canvas vertically. n Clear canvas. Clears any graphics currently displayed on the drawing canvas. n Undo. Undoes the last action that you performed in the Paint Editor. n Redo. Redoes the last undone action.

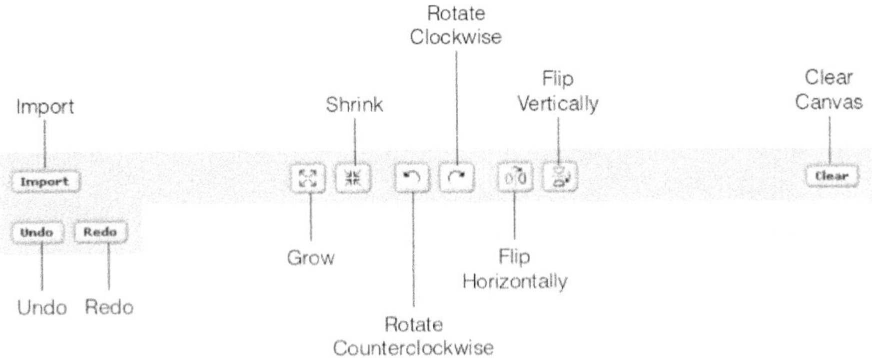

Figure 2.22
The Paint Editor provides access to key functionality through various button controls.

Specifying Color Settings The Paint Editor lets you specify current color settings for both foreground and background drawings using the current Color Settings control located on the lefthand side of the Paint Editor window, just under the options area. To set the current foreground color, click on the top square and then select a color from one of the color palettes that are displayed beneath the control. Likewise, you can set the current background color by selecting the bottom square and then selecting a color from one of the color palettes. Configuring a Sprite's Rotation Center One final but very important Paint Editor feature that you need to know how to use is the Set Rotation Center button located in the lower-left corner of the Paint Editor window. When clicked, this button displays a set of cross-hairs on the Paint Editor's drawing canvas, as demonstrated in Figure 2.23. You can then use drag and drop to move the cross-hair over the portion of the sprite that you want to set up as the sprite's rotational center when the sprite is rotated on the stage.

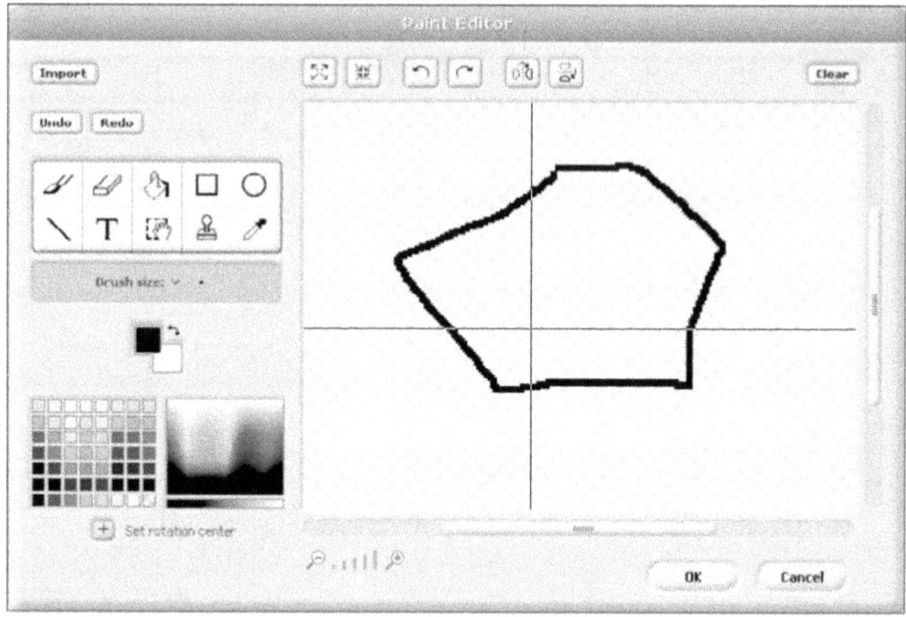

Figure 2.23
Cross-hairs make it easy to set a sprite's rotational center.

The sprite shown in Figure 2.23 is that of a rock that might be used in a space shooter game like Asteroids. In this type of game, the asteroid would move around the screen, threatening to destroy the player's ship by colliding with it. To provide a realistic look and feel, you might want to tell Scratch to rotate the rock as its moves around the screen. By setting up the rock's rotation point as the center of the sprite, it will appear to rotate or spin around its center. On the other hand, by settings its rotation point to be one of the edges of the rock, you can make it rotate in a more wobbly manner.

Summary

This chapter has introduced you to the Scratch IDE and provided a step-by-step overview of all of its major components and functionality. You learned how to work with its menu and toolbar buttons. You learned how to add and delete sprites as well as how to add scripts, costumes, and sounds to sprites. This chapter explained the coordinate system used to control the placement of sprites on the stage. On top of all this, this chapter also provided an overview of Scratch's Paint Editor program and outlined all of its major features and functionality.

CHAPTER FOUR

Basic Components of Scratch Projects

As you have already seen, Scratch application projects are comprised of backgrounds and sprites. Sprites interact and move about the stage under the programmatic control of scripts made up of code blocks. This chapter will explain the three basic types of code blocks and how they work together to create scripts. It will also review the eight categories into which all Scratch's 100-plus code blocks are grouped. Although this chapter does not offer an in-depth review of each individual code block, it will provide a series of tables that you can bookmark and use as a quick reference when developing new Scratch applications.

An overview of the major topics covered in this chapter includes:

- A detailed explanation of stack blocks, hat blocks, and reporter blocks

- A demonstration of how to work with and configure monitors

- A review of all 100-plus code blocks that make up Scratch scripts

- An explanation of how to display help information for individual code blocks

Working with Blocks and Stacks

To bring the backgrounds and sprites that make up Scratch applications to life, you must create scripts. Scripts are created by dragging and dropping code blocks from the blocks palette to the scripts area and snapping them together, creating

53

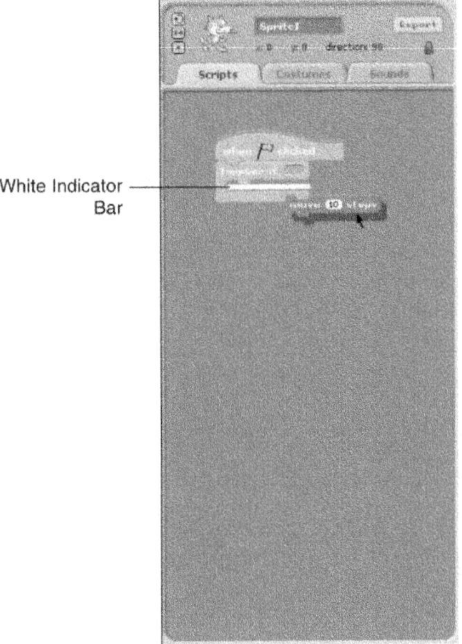

Figure 3.1
Use the visual indicator to determine valid connection points.

stacks. Scripts can be run by double-clicking on one of the code blocks. Scripts can also be configured to automatically execute when predefined events occur.

You can drag a code block around the scripts area. As demonstrated in Figure 3.1, when you drag a block near other blocks, a white indicator bar appears to designate locations where a valid connection can be made. Code blocks can be snapped to the top and bottom of stacks or inserted into the middle of the stack.

You can move code stacks by clicking on their uppermost blocks and dragging them to a new location. If you drag a block from the middle of a stack, all of the code blocks underneath it are dragged out as well.

Tip

You can copy a stack of code blocks from one sprite to another by dragging and dropping the stack onto the thumbnail of a sprite located in the sprite list.

Three Basic Types of Scratch Blocks

Scratch applications are made up of sprites that interact with one another and the user. Sprites are controlled and animated by scripts. Sprites can have any number of scripts, each of which is designed to perform a specific task or action. Scripts are made up of one of more Scratch code blocks. In total, there are more than 100 different Scratch blocks, each of which is designed to fulfill a specific purpose. These blocks can be broadly classified into three categories, as outlined here:

- Stack blocks

- Hat blocks

- Reporter blocks

Working with Stack Blocks

The majority of code blocks provided by Scratch are stack blocks. *Stack blocks* are code blocks with a notch at the top or a bump at the bottom. The notches and bumps serve as visual indicators that identify how the blocks can be snapped together to create programming logic. Figure 3.2 shows an example of a typical stack block.

The notch on the top indicates that the code block can be attached to the underside of another code block. The bump at the bottom of the code block allows other code blocks to attach to its underside. Figure 3.3 shows an example of another stack block. This block will repeatedly execute any code blocks that you choose to embed inside it for as long as a tested condition evaluates as true.

Note

You will learn about the application of repetitive and conditional programming logic in Chapter 9.

Figure 3.2
An example of a code block that is used to halt the playback of an audio file.

Figure 3.3
This code block allows other stack blocks to be embedded within it.

Some stack blocks include an input area inside them that allows you to specify a value by typing in a number. For example, the stack block shown in Figure 3.4 lets you assign the color to be used when drawing by inserting a color-associated numeric value.

To modify the value assigned to a block like the one shown in Figure 3.4, click on the white area within the code block and type in a new value. Some code blocks

Figure 3.4
This code block is used to specify the color to be used when drawing.

Figure 3.5
This code block has a pull-down menu that you can use to configure how it operates.

let you configure them by selecting a value from a pull-down list, as demonstrated in Figure 3.5.

Working with Hat Blocks

A *hat block* is a code block with a rounded or curved top and a bump at the bottom, visually indicating that it can be snapped on top of other stack blocks. Hat blocks provide the ability to create event-driven scripts. An *event-driven* script is one that automatically executes when a specified event occurs. An example of an event that can automatically trigger script execution is when the user clicks on the green flag button. When this event occurs, any scripts that begin with the hat block shown in Figure 3.6 are automatically executed.

Script execution can also be triggered when the user clicks on a sprite. This can be set up by adding the code block shown in Figure 3.7 to the beginning of the script.

Note

Every sprite in an application can potentially have its own scripts. You can automate the execution of any or all of the scripts using hat blocks. In addition to sprites, the stage can also have scripts.

Working with Reporter Blocks

A third type of Scratch code block is a reporter block. A *reporter block* is a code block that has either rounded or angled sides and is specifically designed as a mechanism for providing input for other code blocks to process. For example, the code block shown in Figure 3.8 is a typical reporter block.

Figure 3.6
This hat block automatically runs a script when the user clicks on the green flag.

Figure 3.7
This hat block runs a script whenever the user clicks on the sprite to which this script belongs.

Figure 3.8
This code block retrieves a numeric value indicating a sprite's volume.

Figure 3.9
You can provide input to this code block by either keying it in or using a reporter block.

Figure 3.10
Angled report blocks pass Boolean data to other code blocks for processing.

Figure 3.11
This code block pauses script execution until a specified event is true.

Figure 3.12
This particular combination of code blocks will pause script execution until the user presses the spacebar.

As you can see, this reporter block has rounded sides. As such, it can only fit into code blocks like the one shown in Figure 3.9, whose input area displays a shape with rounded sides.

Figure 3.10 shows an example of a reporter block that has angled sides. This particular code block returns a value of true if the user has pressed the spacebar or a false if the spacebar has not been pressed. Because it has angled sides, it can only be embedded inside code blocks that contain an input area whose sides are also angled.

Note

> *Boolean* is a term used to represent data that has one of two values, either true or false.

To take advantage of a reporter block like the one shown in Figure 3.10, you need to embed the reporter block into another code block that has been designed to work with it. For example, Figure 3.11 shows one such code block.

Figure 3.12 demonstrates how a reporter blocks looks after being embedded within another code block.

Keeping an Eye Out with Monitors

You have probably noticed that Scratch displays a small check box just to the left of certain code blocks in the blocks palette, as demonstrated in Figure 3.13.

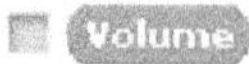

Figure 3.13
An example of a code block capable of displaying a monitor on the stage.

Figure 3.14
By default, a monitor displays the name of its associated code block.

Figure 3.15
Monitors can be configured to display a large readout.

Figure 3.16
Variable monitors also support a display format that includes a slider bar.

The presence of a check box indicates that the code block is capable of displaying a monitor on the stage. A *monitor* is a small block that displays the value currently assigned to the code block. To display the monitor, just click on the check box to select it. When you do so, a gray block is automatically displayed on the stage, as demonstrated in Figure 3.14.

You can modify the way the monitor looks by right-clicking on it and selecting Large Readout from the popup menu that appears. As a result, the appearance of the monitor will change, as demonstrated in Figure 3.15.

Tip

You can also toggle between monitor formats by double-clicking on the monitor.

Variable-based monitors support a third format, which includes a slider bar, as demonstrated in Figure 3.16. You will learn about variables and their use in Chapter 7, "Storing and Retrieving Data."

Eight Categories of Scratch Blocks

Scratch provides access to over 100 code blocks. These code blocks are organized into eight categories and are made available on the blocks palette. Each of these categories of code blocks is described in the following list:

- **Motion.** Code blocks that control sprite placement, direction, rotation, and movement.

- **Looks.** Code blocks that affect sprite and background appearance and provide the ability to display text.

- **Sound.** Code blocks that control the playback and volume of musical notes and audio files.

- **Pen.** Code blocks that can be used to draw using different colors and pen sizes.

- **Control.** Code blocks that trigger script execution based on predefined events, repeatedly execute programming logic using loops, and perform conditional logic.

- **Sensing.** Code blocks that can be used to determine the location of the mouse-pointer, its distance from other sprites, and whether a sprite is touching another sprite.

- **Numbers.** Code blocks that perform logical comparisons, rounding, and other arithmetic operations.

- **Variables.** Code blocks that can be used to store data used by applications when they execute.

You can view the code blocks belonging to a given category by clicking on one of the eight labeled button controls at the top of the blocks palette. Note that each category of code block is color coded, making it easy to distinguish between code blocks from different categories.

Each of these categories of code blocks is reviewed in the sections that follow. This review covers Scratch's entire collection of code blocks, indicating which ones support monitors and providing a brief description of each block's usage.

Moving Objects Around the Drawing Canvas

Motion blocks control a sprite's placement on the stage. Motion blocks are colored blue. There are motion blocks that let you set the direction a sprite will move and then other blocks to move them. There are also motions blocks that report on a sprite's location and direction. Table 3.1 outlines all of the code blocks that fit into this category.

Table 3.1 Scratch Motion Blocks

Block	Monitor	Description
move 10 steps	No	Moves a sprite forward or backwards a specified number of steps.
turn ↻ 15 degrees	No	Rotates a sprite a specified number of degrees in a clockwise direction.
turn ↺ 15 degrees	No	Rotates a sprite a specified number of degrees in a counterclockwise direction.
point in direction 90 ▾	No	Points a sprite toward a specified direction (0 = up, 90 = right, −90 = left, 180 = down).
point towards	No	Points a sprite toward either the mouse-pointer or a specified sprite.
go to x: 0 y: 0	No	Moves a sprite to a specified coordination location on the stage.
go to	No	Moves a sprite to the location of either the mouse-pointer or another sprite.
glide 1 secs to x: 0 y: 0	No	Moves a sprite to the specified coordinate position over a specified number of seconds.
change x by 10	No	Changes the position of a sprite on the X-axis by a specified number of pixels.
set x to 0	No	Changes a sprite's location on the X-axis to a specified value.
change y by 10	No	Changes the position of a sprite on the Y-axis by a specified number of pixels.
set y to 0	No	Changes a sprite's location on the Y-axis to a specified value.
if on edge, bounce	No	Changes a sprite's direction when it makes contact with one of the edges of the stage.
x position	Yes	Retrieves a value representing a sprite's coordinate on the X-axis (between −240 and 240).
y position	Yes	Retrieves a value representing a sprite's coordinate on the Y-axis (between −180 and 180).
direction	Yes	Retrieves a value representing a sprite's current direction (0 = up, 90 = right, −90 = left, 180 = down).

You will learn more about motion blocks in Chapter 5, "Moving Things Around."

Changing Object Appearance

Looks blocks modify sprite and background appearance and display text within popup bubbles. Looks blocks are colored purple. There are looks blocks that let

Table 3.2 Scratch Looks Blocks

Block	Monitor	Description
switch to costume costume2	No	Changes a sprite's costume, modifying its appearance.
next costume	No	Changes a sprite's costume to the next costume in the sprite's costume list, jumping back to the beginning of the list when the end of the list is reached.
costume #	Yes	Retrieves a numeric value representing a sprite's current costume number.
say Hello! for 2 secs	No	Displays a text message in a speech bubble for a specified number of seconds.
say Hello!	No	Displays a text message in a speech bubble or removes the display of a speech bubble when no text is specified.
think Hmm… for 2 secs	No	Displays a text message in a thought bubble for a specified number of seconds.
think Hmm…	No	Displays a text message in a thought bubble or removes the display of a thought bubble when no text is specified.
change color effect by 25	No	Modifies a sprite's appearance by applying and modifying a special effect (color, fisheye, whirl, pixelate, mosaic, brightness, or ghost) by a specified numeric value.
set color effect to 0	No	Applies a special effect (color, fisheye, whirl, pixelate, mosaic, brightness, or ghost) to a sprite by a specified numeric value.
clear graphic effects	No	Restores a sprite to its normal appearance, removing any special effects that may have been applied.

Table 3.2   (Continued)

Block	Monitor	Description
change size by 10	No	Modifies the size of a sprite by a specified numeric amount.
set size to 100 %	No	Sets a sprite's size to a percentage of its original size.
size	Yes	Retrieves a percentage value representing a sprite's current size when compared to its original size.
show	No	Tells Scratch to display a sprite.
hide	No	Suppresses the display of a sprite on the stage, preventing it from interacting with other sprites.
go to front	No	Places a sprite on top of other sprites, placing it on the top layer and ensuring its display.
go back 1 layers	No	Moves a sprite back a specified number of layers, allowing other sprites to be displayed on top of it.
switch to background background1	No	Alters the stage's appearance by assigning it a different background.
next background	No	Changes the stage's background to the next background in the background list.
background #	No	Retrieves a numeric value representing the background number of the stage's current background.

you modify sprite costumes and colors. There are also blocks that let you modify a sprite's size and control whether a sprite is visible on the stage. Table 3.2 outlines all of the code blocks that fit into this category.

You will learn more about looks blocks in Chapter 10, "Changing the Way Sprites Look and Behave."

Making Some Noise

Sound blocks play music and add sound effects to your Scratch application projects. Sound blocks are colored pink. There are sound blocks that let you play sounds and drum beats, select different types of instruments, control playback volume, and modify tempo. Table 3.3 outlines all of the code blocks that fit into this category.

Table 3.3 Scratch Sound Blocks

Block	Monitor	Description
play sound meow	No	Plays the specified sound file while allowing the script file in which it is inserted to keep executing.
play sound meow until done	No	Plays the specified sound file, pausing script execution until the sound file has finished playing.
stop all sounds	No	Halts the playback of any sound files currently being played.
play drum 48 for 0.2 beats	No	Plays a drum sound selected from the block's pull-down menu a specified number of seconds.
rest for 0.2 beats	No	Pauses sound playback for a specified number of beats.
play note 60 for 0.5 beats	No	Plays a musical note selected from the block's pull-down menu a specified number of beats.
set instrument to 1	No	Specifies the instrument to be used when playing musical notes.
change volume by -10	No	Changes a sprite's volume by a specified value.
set volume to 100 %	No	Sets a sprite's sound volume to a specified percentage level.
volume	Yes	Retrieves a numeric value representing a sprite's sound volume.
change tempo by 20	No	Alters a sprite's tempo by a specified number of beats per minute.
set tempo to 60 bpm	No	Assigns the number of beats per minute to be used as a sprite's tempo.
tempo	Yes	Retrieves a numeric value representing a sprite's tempo.

You will learn more about sound blocks in Chapter 11, "Spicing Things Up with Sounds."

Drawing Lines and Shapes

Pen blocks draw any combination of shapes and lines using a virtual pen. Pen blocks are colored mint green. There are pen blocks that let you enable and disable drawing, set color and pen size, and apply shading. Table 3.4 outlines all of the code blocks that fit into this category.

You will learn more about pen blocks in Chapter 12, "Drawing Lines and Shapes."

Table 3.4 Scratch Pen Blocks

Block	Monitor	Description
clear	No	Erases or clears away anything drawn by the pen or stamped from the stage.
pen down	No	Places the pen in a down position, allowing drawing operations to occur as the pen is moved around the stage.
pen up	No	Disables drawing operations by lifting the pen.
set pen color to	No	Specifies the color to be used when drawing.
change pen color by 10	No	Changes the color used when drawing by a specified amount.
set pen color to 0	No	Specifies the color to be used when drawing based on a numeric range in which 0 is red (at the low end of the spectrum) and 100 equals blue (at the high end of the spectrum).
change pen shade by 10	No	Modifies the shading used when drawing by a specified amount.
set pen shade to 50	No	Specifies the shade to be used when drawing based on a numeric range in which 0 is the darkest possible shading and 100 represents the maximum possible amount of light.
change pen size by 1	No	Modifies the thickness of the pen based on a numeric increment.
set pen size to 1	No	Specifies the thickness or width of the pen used when drawing.
stamp	No	Draws or stamps the image of a sprite onto the stage.

Looping, Conditional Logic, and Event Programming

Control blocks automate the execution of scripts, pause script execution, and send messages to other sprites, allowing sprites to synchronize their execution. There are also control blocks that let you set up loops to repeatedly execute collections of code blocks as well as control blocks that let you conditionally execute other code blocks based on whether or not a test condition evaluates as true. Control blocks are colored gold. Table 3.5 outlines all of the code blocks that fit into this category.

You will learn more about control blocks in Chapter 9.

Sensing Sprite Location and Environmental Input

Sensing blocks determine the location of the mouse-pointer, its distance from other sprites, and whether a sprite is touching another sprite. Sensing blocks are

Table 3.5 Scratch Control Blocks

Block	Monitor	Description
when [green flag] clicked	No	Executes the script to which it has been attached whenever the IDE's green flag button is pressed.
when [space] key pressed	No	Executes the script to which it has been attached whenever a specified keyboard key is pressed.
when Sprite1 clicked	No	Executes the script to which it has been attached whenever the user clicks on the sprite to which the script belongs.
wait 1 secs	No	Pauses script execution for a specified number of seconds, after which the script resumes its execution.
forever	No	Repeatedly executes all of the code blocks embedded inside it.
repeat 10	No	Repeats the execution of all the code blocks embedded inside it a specified number of times.
broadcast	No	Specifies a broadcast message to all sprites without pausing script execution.
broadcast and wait	No	Sends a broadcast message to all sprites to trigger a predefined action and then pauses script execution, waiting until all sprites have completed their assigned action before allowing the script in which the block resides to continue executing.
when I receive	No	Executes the scripts to which it has been attached when a specified broadcast message is received.
forever if	No	Repeatedly executes all of the code blocks embedded within the control for as long as the specified condition evaluates as true.
if	No	Executes all of the code blocks embedded within the control if the specified condition evaluates as true.
if else	No	Executes all of the code blocks embedded in the top half of the control (between the If an Else) if the specified condition evaluates as true and executes all of the code blocks embedded in the bottom half of the control (after Else) if the condition evaluates as being false.
wait until	No	Pauses script execution until a specified condition becomes true.
repeat until	No	Repeats all of the code blocks embedded inside it for as long as a tested condition evaluates as true.

Table 3.5 (Continued)

Block	Monitor	Description
stop script	No	Halts a script's execution.
stop all	No	Halts the execution of all scripts for all sprites in the application.

colored sky blue. There are sensing blocks that can be used to interact with Scratch boards, allowing applications to detect when the sensor board's buttons or slider are being pressed. Table 3.6 outlines all of the code blocks that fit into this category.

Note

A *Scratch board* is a special piece of hardware that you can purchase from the Scratch website and attach to your computer. Once it is attached, you can use a sensor board to collect and process environment- and user-provided input. You will learn how to programmatically interact with and control Scratch boards in Chapter 14, "Collecting External Input Using a Scratch Sensor Board."

You will learn more about sensing blocks in Chapter 6, "Sensing Sprite Position and Controlling Environmental Settings."

Working with Numbers

Numbers blocks perform arithmetic operations, generate random numbers, and compare numeric values to determine their relationship to one another. Numbers blocks are green. There are numbers blocks that can be used to round numeric values and to execute a host of mathematical functions like determining absolute value or square root of a number. Table 3.7 outlines all of the code blocks that fit into this category.

You will learn more about number blocks in Chapter 8, "Doing a Little Math."

Storing and Retrieving Data

Variables blocks store and retrieve numeric values in computer memory. You will need to use variables to store data as your application executes. For example, if you create a game that challenges the player to try and guess a randomly

Table 3.6 Scratch Sensing Blocks

Block	Monitor	Description
mouse x	No	Retrieves the location of the mouse-pointer on the X-axis.
mouse y	No	Retrieves the location of the mouse-pointer on the Y-axis.
mouse down?	No	Retrieves a Boolean value of true or false, depending on whether a mouse button is pressed.
key space pressed?	No	Retrieves a Boolean value of true or false, depending on whether a specified key is pressed.
touching ?	No	Retrieves a Boolean value of true or false, depending on whether the sprite is touching a specified sprite, edge, or mouse-pointer as selected from the block's pull-down menu.
touching color ?	No	Retrieves a Boolean value of true of false, depending on whether the sprite is touching a specified color.
color is touching ?	No	Retrieves a Boolean value of true of false, depending on whether the first specified color inside the sprite is touching the second specified color on the background or on another sprite.
distance to	No	Retrieves a numeric value representing a sprite's distance from another sprite or from the mouse-pointer.
reset timer	No	Resets the timer back to its default value of zero.
timer	Yes	Retrieves a numeric value representing the number of seconds that the timer has run.
x position of Sprite1	No	Retrieves the property value (x position, y position, direction, customer #, and size of volume) for the background of a specified sprite.
loudness	Yes	Retrieves a numeric value, from 1 to 100, representing the volume of the computer's microphone.
loud?	Yes	Retrieves a Boolean value of true or false when a sound value of 30 or greater is detected through the computer's microphone.
slider sensor value	Yes	Retrieves the value being reported by one of the sensors on a Scratch board.
sensor button pressed ?	Yes	Retrieves a Boolean value of true or false, depending on whether a specified sensor is being pressed.

generated number, you will need to use a variable to store and refer back to this number.

Variables can be used in conjunction with conditional programming logic to control the execution of other code blocks. Variables can also be used to control

Table 3.7 Scratch Numbers Blocks

Block	Monitor	Description
	No	Adds two numbers together and generates a result.
	No	Subtracts one number from another and returns the result.
	No	Multiplies two numbers together and generates a result.
	No	Divides one number into another and returns the result.
pick random 1 to 10	No	Generates a random number within the specified range.
	No	Returns a Boolean value of true or false, depending on whether one number is less than another.
	No	Returns a Boolean value of true or false, depending on whether one number is equal to another.
	No	Returns a Boolean value of true or false, depending on whether one number is greater than another.
and	No	Returns a Boolean value of true or false, depending on whether two separately evaluated conditions are both true.
or	No	Returns a Boolean value of true or false, depending on whether either of two separately evaluated conditions is true.
not	No	Reverses the Boolean value from true to false or false to true.
mod	No	Retrieves the remainder portion of a division operation between two numbers.
round	No	Returns the nearest integer value for a specified number.
sqrt of 10	No	Returns the result of the selected function (abs, sqrt, sin, cos, tan, asin, acos, atan, Ln, log, E^, and 10^) when applied to the specified number.

the repeated execution of code blocks embedded within code block loops. Variables blocks are colored orange. You can create and name custom variables blocks and assign them a starting value. You can also modify their values during script execution. Other code blocks can retrieve variable values and use them as input. Table 3.8 outlines all of the code blocks that fit into this category.

You will learn more about variables blocks in Chapter 7.

Table 3.8 Scratch Variables Blocks

Block	Monitor	Description
change PlayerScore by 1	No	Modifies the value assigned to a numeric value stored in a variable by the specified amount.
set PlayerScore to 0	No	Assigns a value to a numeric variable.
PlayerScore	Yes	Retrieves the value assigned to a variable.

Getting Help with Code Blocks

In addition to bookmarking and referring back to the tables provided in this chapter to find out what a given code block does, you can view help information for any Scratch code block by right-clicking on the code block in the blocks palette, as demonstrated in Figure 3.17.

Alternatively, you can right-click on a code block once it has been added to the scripts area to access a link to the block's help file, as demonstrated in Figure 3.18.

By clicking on the Help link in the popup menu that is displayed, you can display help information for that control. For example, Figure 3.19 shows the help information that is available for the forever code block.

As Figure 3.19 shows, the help information that is displayed explains the purpose of the code block and demonstrates its usage.

Figure 3.17
Accessing help for a given Scratch code block.

Figure 3.18
Accessing help for a Scratch code block that has been added to the scripts area.

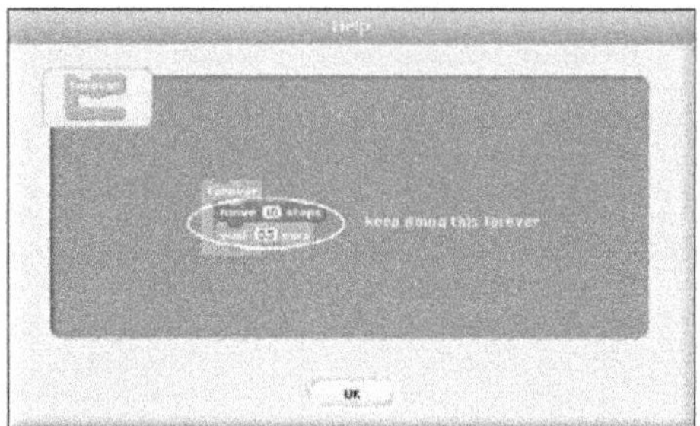

Figure 3.19
Displaying the help window for the `forever` code block.

Summary

This chapter provided a quick reference that outlined the purpose and usage of all of the code blocks provided by Scratch. You may want to bookmark this chapter to help make it easy to return to and take advantage of this information. This chapter explained the three types of code blocks supported by Scratch and outlined their relationship to one another. The chapter then provided an explanation of all 100 plus Scratch code blocks, going over them category by category. On top of all this, you learned how to work with and configure monitors and to access help information for individual code blocks.

CHAPTER FIVE

Quick Scratch Project

So far, you have been presented with an overview of Scratch and its capabilities and learned how to work with its IDE. You have also been given an overview of all of the code blocks that make up the Scratch programming language and learned the basic steps involved in creating Scratch applications. Now that you are more familiar with Scratch and its key components, let's put this new knowledge to use by creating a new Scratch application project, examining in greater detail the steps involved in creating and executing Scratch applications. The topics covered in this chapter include: n A review of the programming concepts that Scratch can teach you n A detailed overview of how to build Scratch applications n Learning how to distribute your Scratch programs on CD-ROM Programming with Scratch As a beginner's programming language, Scratch teaches you a number of critical programming concepts that you will be able to later rely on should you decide to make the jump to other more traditional and industrial-strength programming languages like Microsoft Visual Basic, Cþþ, JavaScript, and AppleScript. The programming concepts that you can learn from Scratch include: n Sequential Processing. This involves the processing of application code blocks, in the order that they are laid out, starting at the beginning of a script file and continuing to the end of the script. n Conditional Programming Logic. This involves the conditional execution of code blocks based on data collected during application execution. n Use of Variables. This involves the storage, retrieval, and modification of data during application execution. n Iterative Processing. This involves the repeated execution of code blocks to process large amounts of information or to control the repeated execution of code blocks required to direct the execution of a game or application. n Boolean Logic. This involves the application of programming logic that executes based on the analysis of true/false data provided by Scratch during program execution. n Interface Design. This involves the development of user-friendly and intuitive application stage layout, making it easy for users to interact with applications. n Program Synchronization. This involves the passage and receipt of messages between application scripts for the purpose of coordinating the execution of different parts of an application. n Event Handling. This involves the initiation of script execution based on the occurrence of predefined events, such as the pressing of keyboard keys, the pressing of the green flag key, or the receipt of a synchronization message. n Application and Game Development. This involves the creation of different types of computer application projects. n Sprite Programming. This involves the use of sprites as the basis for developing graphical programs. n Application Troubleshooting. This involves the identification, location, and elimination of programming errors, or bugs, that prevent applications from executing as they are supposed to. 74 Chapter 4 n Mr. Wiggly's Dance—A Quick Scratch Project You will learn more about each of these programming concepts as you make your way through the remainder of this book. Note As powerful and fun as Scratch is, there are some programming concepts that it does not teach. These concepts include the storage of collections of data in arrays, the ability to process file input and output, the ability to organize application code into procedures, and the ability to support advanced object-oriented programming techniques. However, as a first-time programmer, these concepts can be challenging to learn, and by omitting them, the developers of Scratch have produced a streamlined yet powerful learning environment, which will prepare you to later make the jump to programming languages that support these advanced programming concepts. Creating the Mr. Wiggly's Dance Application The rest of this chapter is dedicated to leading you through the development of the Mr. Wiggly's Dance application. In this Scratch application, a short, round, and comical cartoonish character named Mr. Wiggly dances around the stage to music, as demonstrated in Figure 4.1. Because Mr. Wiggly is bashful, his skin changes color as he dances, as demonstrated in Figure 4.2. Although not immediately obvious when viewed in black and white, if you compare the color of Mr. Wiggly in Figures 4.1 and 4.2, you will notice that he has definitely begun to blush, betraying his discomfort at dancing in front of an audience. Creating the Mr. Wiggly's Dance Appl

Figure 4.1
Mr. Wiggly practices his dance moves, dancing back and forth across the stage.

Figure 4.2
The bashful Mr. Wiggly's skin color changes as he dances.

Figure 4.3
Mr. Wiggly pauses at the end of each dance only to decide to keep dancing.

At the end of each dance, Mr. Wiggly pauses for a moment to reflect on how things are going before deciding to keep on dancing, as demonstrated in Figure 4.3. The Mr. Wiggly's Dance application project will be created by following a series of steps, as outlined here:

1. Creating a new Scratch application project.
2. Adding a project background.
3. Adding and removing sprites to and from the project.
4. Importing a music file into the application.
5. Scripting audio playback.
6. Adding the programming logic required to make Mr. Wiggly dance.
7. Saving and executing your work.

Since this book has yet to provide a detailed explanation of how to work with all of the Scratch code blocks used in this application project, brief explanations will be provided. You will learn the ins and out of programming with code blocks in Chapters 5 through 12. As you make your way through each of the steps in this project, try and keep your focus on the overall process being followed and do not get caught up in the specifics. Later, once you have finished reviewing Chapters 5 through 12, you can always return and review this project again and clear up any questions you may have.

Step 1: Creating a New Scratch Project The first step in creating a Scratch project is to start Scratch. Doing so results in the automatic creation of a new Scratch project. New Scratch projects come equipped with a single sprite with two costumes representing a cat. You can choose to incorporate this sprite into your application or to remove it. If, on the other hand, Scratch has already been started and you have been working with it for a while, you can create and open a new Scratch application project by clicking on the New button located on the Scratch menu bar. In response, a new project is opened in the IDE, as shown in Figure 4.4.

Step 2: Adding a Background to the Stage With your new Scratch application project now created, it is time to get to work. Let's begin by adding a suitable background to the stage that will help set the mood of the application. Backgrounds are associated with the stage, so to add a background to your application, you must click on the blank stage thumbnail located in the sprite list. Once selected, the stage thumbnail is highlighted with a blue outline, as shown in Figure 4.5. Once you have selected the stage thumbnail, you can modify its background by clicking on the Backgrounds tab located at the top of the scripts area. When you do so, the currently assigned stage background is displayed, as shown in Figure 4.6.

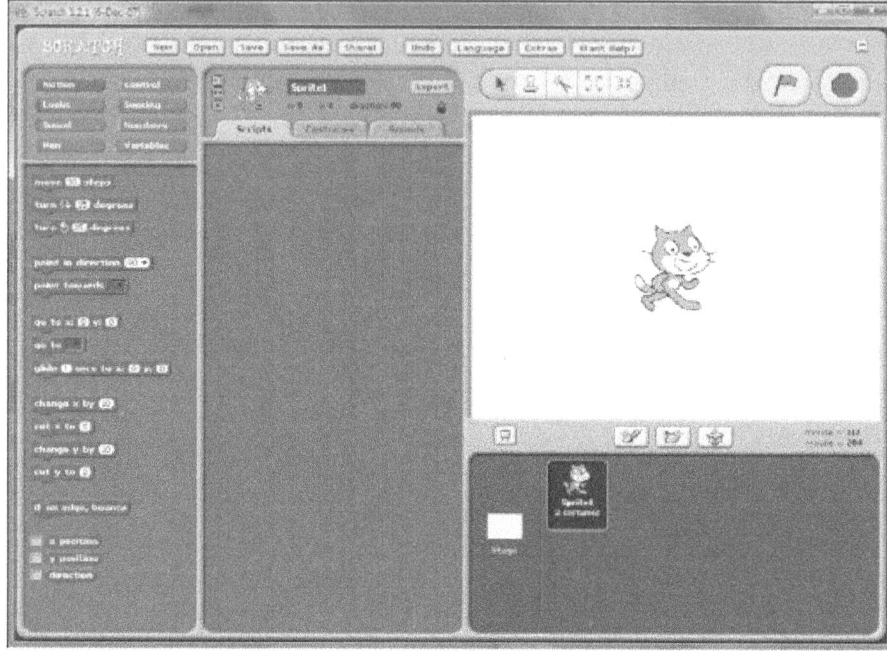

Figure 4.4
New Scratch application projects come supplied with a single sprite.

Figure 4.5
Selected thumbnails in the sprite list are highlighted with a blue outline.

To replace the currently assigned blank background with something more interesting, click on the Import button. This will open the Import Background window. Once opened, click on the Indoors folder, select the chalkboard thumbnail, as shown in Figure 4.7, and click on the OK button.

Figure 4.6
The Backgrounds tab provides the ability to create, import, edit, and rename backgrounds.

Figure 4.7
Importing a new background into your Scratch application project.

Once imported, the new background will be added to the application's current list of background files, as shown in Figure 4.8. As you can see, the thumbnail is automatically assigned a name and a number. Since this application only requires one background, you can remove the default blank background named background1 from your project by clicking on the Delete This Costume button, which is located to the right of the background's picture and represented by a round X button.

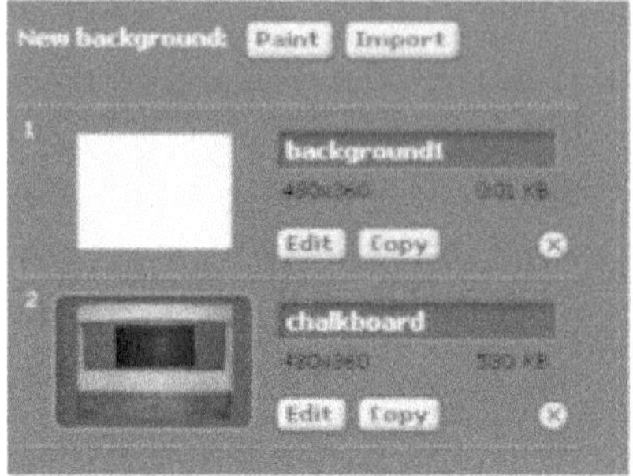

Figure 4.8
Scratch applications can have any number of backgrounds and can switch between them during execution.

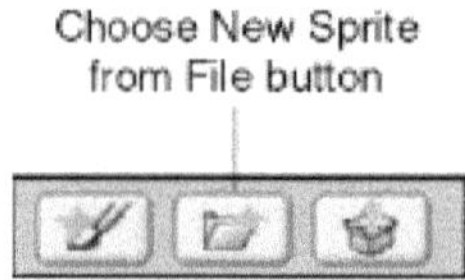

Figure 4.9
Click on the Choose New Sprite from File button to access a collection of ready-made sprites.

Step 3: Adding and Removing Sprites The next step in the development of this Scratch project is to add a sprite representing Mr. Wiggly to the project and to remove the cat sprite, which is not needed in this application. To add the sprite representing Mr. Wiggly, click on the Choose New Sprite from File button, as shown in Figure 4.9. This button is the middle button that makes up the collection of new sprite buttons, located just beneath the stage and just above the sprite list. Scratch provides ready access to all kinds of sprites, organized into the following six folders:

Animals
Fantasy
Letters
People
Things
Transportation

The sprite that you want to use to represent Mr. Wiggly is located in the People folder. Once clicked, the Choose New Sprite from File button instructs Scratch to display the New Sprite window, which provides access to the six folders listed above. Open the People folder and then scroll down until you locate the roundman sprite, as shown in Figure 4.10. Select the roundman sprite by clicking on it and then click on the OK button. The New Sprite window will close and the new sprite will be added to the middle of the stage, as shown in Figure 4.11.

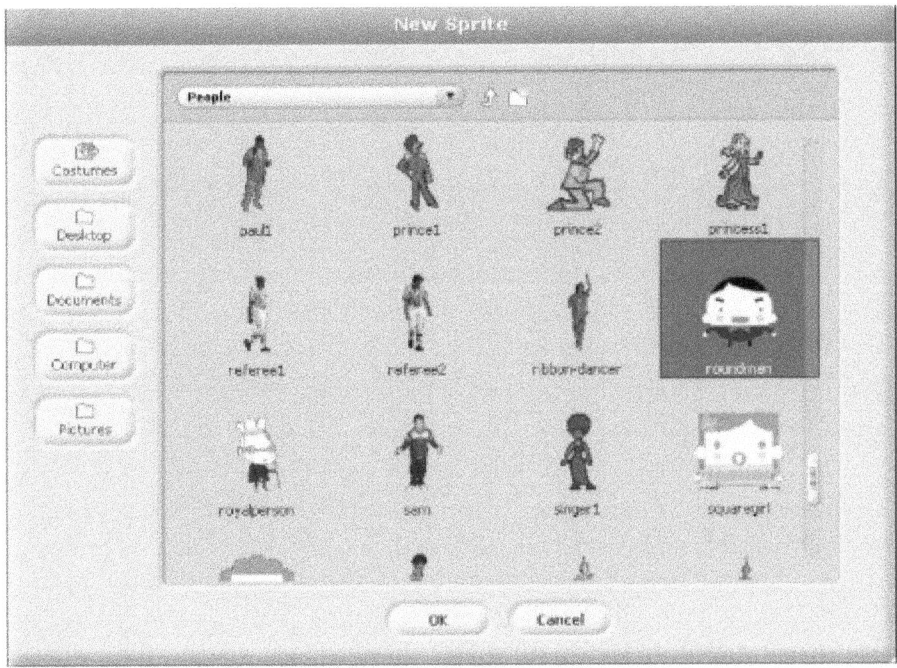

Figure 4.10
Selecting the sprite that will be used to represent Mr Wiggly.

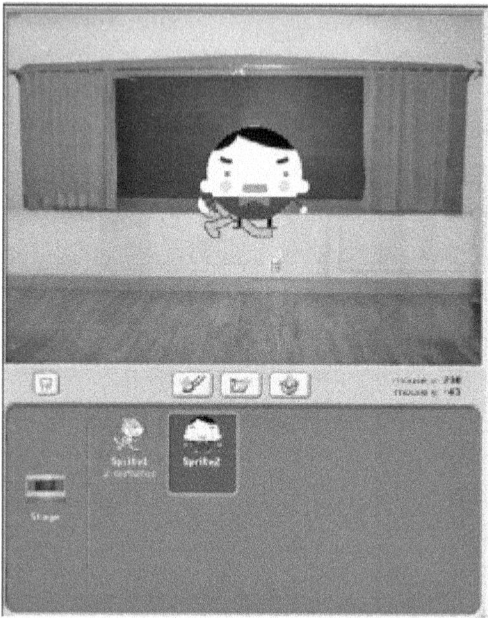

Figure 4.11
A thumbnail representing the sprite is also added to the sprite list.

When contrasted against the stage's background, Mr. Wiggly's default placement in the middle of the stage makes it look like he is floating on air. To put things into proper perspective, drag and drop Mr. Wiggly about one inch lower down the stage, so that it looks like he is standing on the floor. Since the Mr. Wiggly's Dance application does not need the default cat sprite, go ahead and remove this sprite from the application project by selecting the Delete button on the Scratch toolbar and then clicking on the thumbnail for the cat located in the sprite list.

Step 4: Adding Mr. Wiggly's Music Now that you have taken care of the sprites needed by the application, it is time to import the sound file. To do this, click on the thumbnail representing the stage in the sprite list and then click on the Sounds tab in the scripts area. In response, Scratch will display all of the sound files belonging to the sprite. By default, every

Figure 4.12
All sprites supplied by Scratch come equipped with the same sound file.

sprite in a Scratch application is assigned a common sound file named pop, as shown in Figure 4.12. Scratch provides ready access to all kinds of prerecorded audio files. The name of the sound file that Mr. Wiggly will dance to is Eggs. To add this file to the sprite, click on the Import button. In response, Scratch will display the Import Sound window, which by default contains eight folders, listed next, in which Scratch stores its audio files.

Drill down into the Music Loops folder by double-clicking on it. Locate and click on the Eggs file, as shown in Figure 4.13. Scratch will immediately play the file, so you can hear what it sounds like. Click on the OK button to import the sound file into your application project, as demonstrated in Figure 4.14. Note that for each sound file, a number of pieces of information are displayed. You can see the name of the file, the length of time that it takes to play the file, and the file's size. Note that the Eggs sound file takes

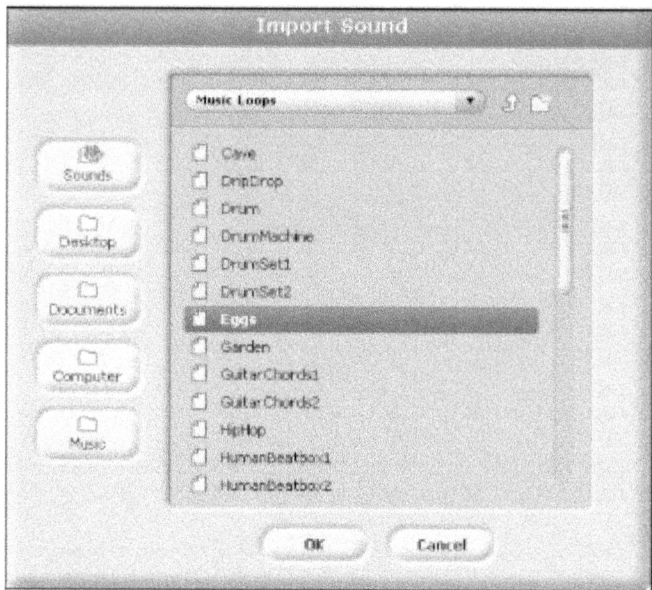

Figure 4.13
Importing a sound file into a Scratch application project.

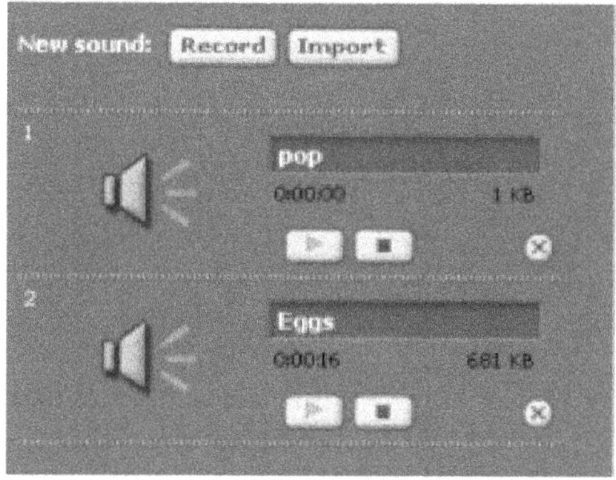

Figure 4.14
You can add any number of sound files to a sprite.

16 second to play. You will need to remember this information a little later when programming the playback of this sound file. The default pop

sound file is not needed by this application; therefore, you can delete it by clicking on the round Delete This Sound button located at the bottom-right side of the sound file entry Step 5: Playing the Dance Music It is time to begin putting together the program code logic required to make your new application work. In total you will need to create two scripts for this project: one for the stage and another for the sprite representing Mr. Wiggly. The script belonging to the stage will be made up of code blocks that are responsible for playing the application's background music. The script belonging to the sprite will contain the programming logic required to make Mr. Wiggly dance. The first step in the development of the stage's script is to click on the Control button in the blocks palette and then to drag and drop an instance of the when green flag clicked block onto the scripts area, as demonstrated in Figure 4.15. This hat code block will automatically execute the script to which it is attached whenever the green flag button is clicked. Since the application's background music is supposed to be played over and over again for as long as the application runs, you need to set up a loop that will repeatedly play the sound file. To set this up, drag and drop an instance of the forever code block to the scripts area, attaching it to the bottom of the when green flag clicked block, as shown in Figure 4.16. Now that you have the loop set up, click on the Sound button located at the top of the blocks palette and then drag and drop an instance of the play sound code block onto the scripts area, embedding it inside the forever code block. Next, click on the pull-down menu located on the right-hand side of the code block and select Eggs from the list that appears. At this point the script that you are developing should look like the example shown in Figure 4.17.

At this point you only need to add one last code block to the script to finish it up. To do so, click on the Control button located at the top of the blocks palette and then drag and drop an instance of the wait secs code block over the scripts area, inserting it inside the forever code block, immediately following the play sound block, as shown in Figure 4.18. This block is needed to pause the loop for 16 seconds, allowing for the complete playback of the sound file, before the loop repeats and begins playing it again.

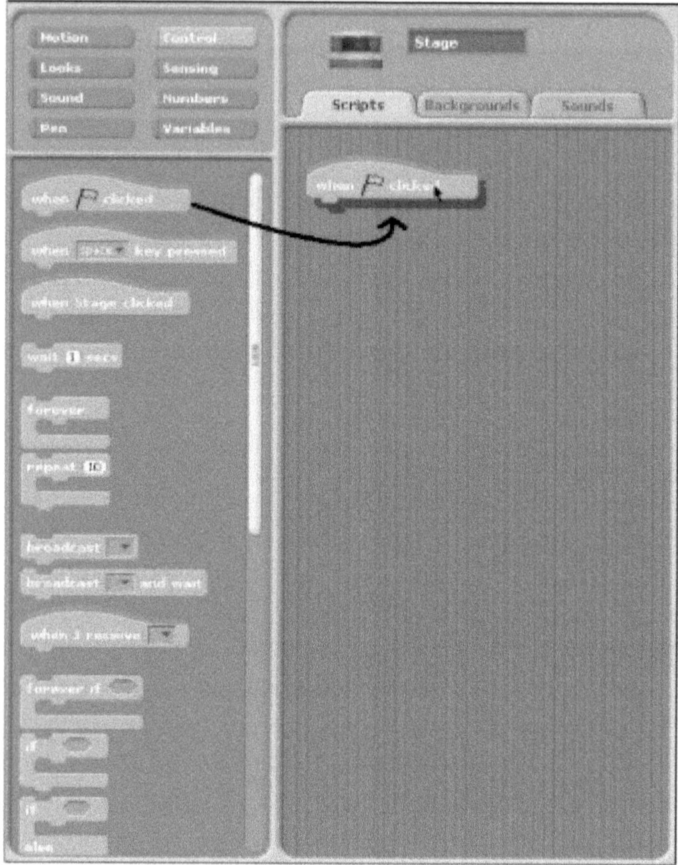

Figure 4.15
This block will be used to automatically execute the script whenever the green flag button is clicked.

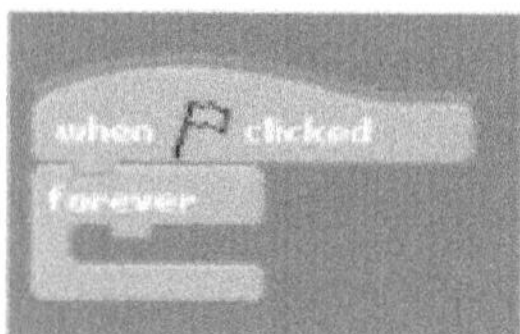

Figure 4.16
The forever block will repeat the execution of any code block that you embed within it.

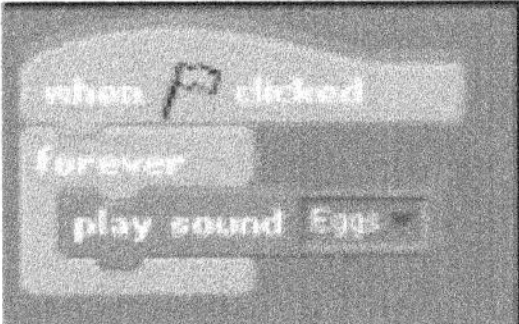

Figure 4.17
Using the play sound code block to play back the Eggs sound file.

Figure 4.18
Pausing loop execution to allow playback of the sound file to complete.

Step 6: Making Mr. Wiggly Dance Now that you have finished work on the stage's script, it is time to write the script that makes Mr. Wiggly dance. To do so, click on the thumbnail of the sprite representing Mr. Wiggly (in the sprite area). In response, Scratch should clear out the script's area and automatically select the Scripts tab for you so that you can begin script development.The first step in the development of this is to click on the Control button in the blocks palette and then to drag and drop an instance of the when green flag clicked block onto the scripts area, as demonstrated in Figure 4.19. This hat code block will automatically execute the script to which it is attached whenever the green flag button is clicked. In this application, Mr. Wiggly is supposed to dance over and over again without stopping (until the user stops running the application). To set this up, drag and drop an instance of the forever code block onto the scripts area and attach it to the bottom of the when green flag clicked block, as shown in Figure 4.20. Next, it is time to add a pair of code statements that will move Mr. Wiggly 25 steps to the right and then pause for two seconds. This is accomplished by dragging and dropping the move steps and wait secs blocks to the scripts area, embedding them inside the forever code block, as shown in Figure 4.21. Note

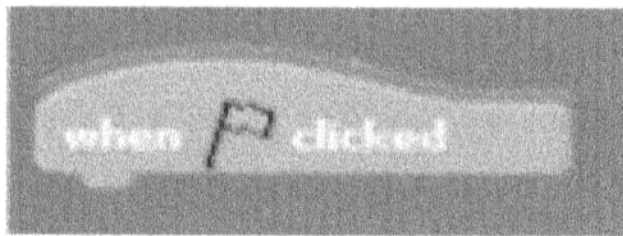

Figure 4.19
Setting up the script to execute when the green flag is clicked.

Figure 4.20
Adding a loop to the script to repeat the execution of embedded code blocks.

Figure 4.21
Adding the programming logic that makes Mr. Wiggly dance his first step.

Figure 4.22
Adding the remaining code blocks required to complete Mr. Wiggly's dance routine.

that by default the move steps block is set to 10. You will need to replace this with a value of 25. Next, you need to add a series of move steps and wait secs code blocks, which, when executed, will move Mr. Wiggly 25 steps to the right followed by four moves to the left at 25 steps each and then another two moves back towards the right. This is accomplished by adding seven sets of a code block, as shown in Figure 4.22. To complete the development of this script, you need to add two looks blocks, as shown in Figure 4.23. The change effect by code block is used to modify Mr. Wiggly's color each time the loop finishes its execution, simulating the feeling of embarrassment that Mr. Wiggly experiences when he dances. Lastly, the think for secs code block is used to display a text message in a popup bubble that shows Mr. Wiggly thinking about and then deciding to keep dancing.

Figure 4.23
Modifying Mr. Wiggly's color and displaying his thoughts.

Step 7: Saving and Executing Your New Scratch Application At this point your copy of the Mr. Wiggly's Dance application should be complete. All that remains is for you to save the application and then to execute it and see how it looks when running. To save your application, click on the Save button located on the IDE's menu bar. In response, Scratch will display the Save Project window, as demonstrated in Figure 4.24, prompting you to specify the name and location where you want to store your new application. In addition, Scratch provides the opportunity to enter your name as the project author and to enter notes describing the project in the Project Author and About This Project text fields. Once you are done, click on the OK button to save your Scratch application project. Once you have saved your work, run the application to see how it works. Since both of the application's scripts are configured to execute whenever the green flag button is pressed, all you have to do is click on that button and sit back and watch as the bashful Mr. Wiggly dances about the stage for your amusement.

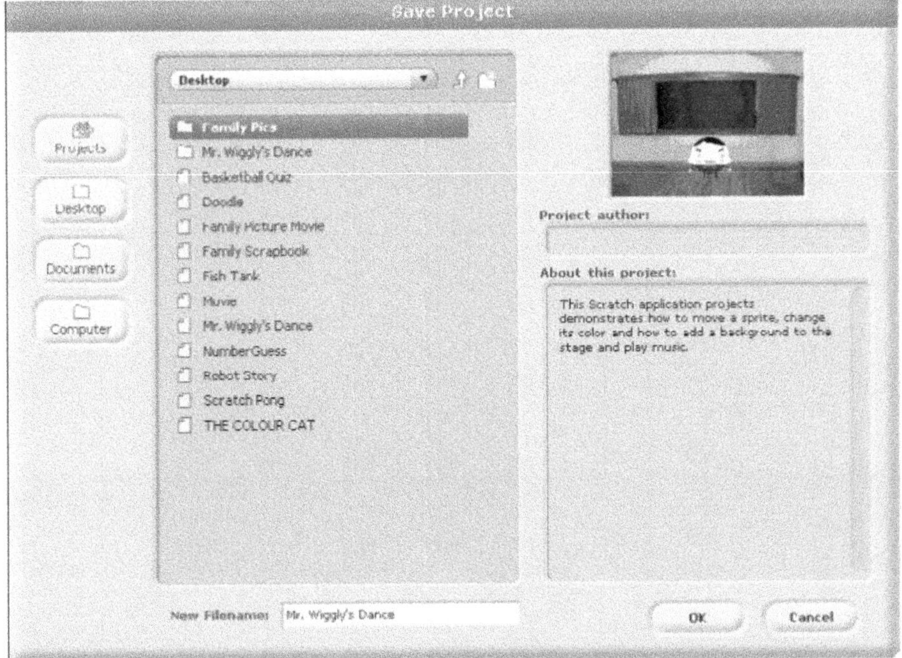

Figure 4.24
Saving your copy of the Mr. Wiggly's Dance application project.

Distributing Scratch Projects Scratch is an interpreted programming language. This means that unlike some programming languages, such as Visual Basic and Cþþ, which compile their applications into an executable file that can then be run on other computers without requiring that the programming language be installed, Scratch applications can only execute when run within the Scratch IDE (or on the Scratch website at http://scratch.mit.edu). Therefore, if you want to distribute your Scratch applications and have them execute on someone else's computer, you must first see to it that Scratch is installed on the other computer, or you must create a special application distribution CD that includes Scratch system files required to run your application when Scratch has not been installed. Note You can also share access to your Scratch application projects by posting them on the Scratch website and pointing your friends to that website, where they can view and run them using a Java-enabled web browser. You will learn all about the steps involved in sharing your Scratch applications this way in Chapter 13, "Sharing Your Scratch Projects Over the Internet."

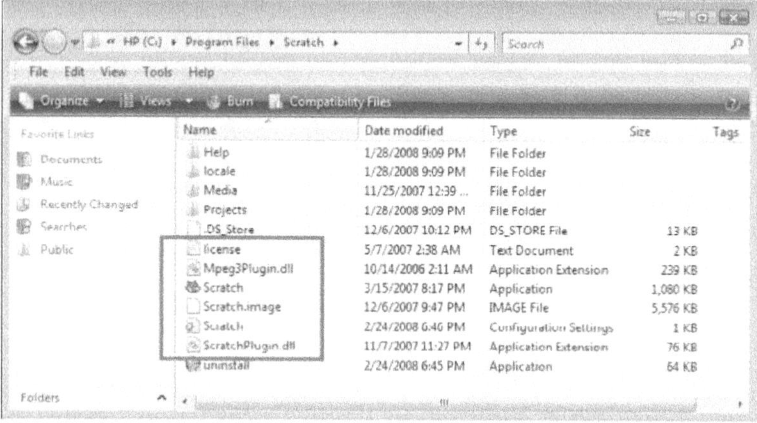

Figure 4.25
Burn a copy of the files shown in this figure along with your Scratch application file to create a distributable Windows CD-ROM.

Distributing Scratch Applications to Windows Computers The files that you need to burn to your distribution CD-ROM vary, depending on whether you are working with Microsoft Windows or Mac OS X. When working with Microsoft Windows, you will need to burn the following files identified in Figure 4.25, as well as a copy of your Scratch application, to a CD-ROM. Each of the files listed can be found in the folder in which you installed Scratch, which on Microsoft Windows is C:\Program Files\Scratch by default.

Scratch.exe
Scratch.image
Scratch.ini
ScratchPlugin.dll
Mpeg3Plugin.dll
License.txt

Distributing Scratch Applications to Mac OS X Computers If you are working with Mac OS X and want to create a distribution disc to share your creations with other Mac users who do not have Scratch installed on their computers, you may do so by burning a CD-ROM containing your Scratch application projects as well as the following Scratch system files, all of which are available in Scratch's installation folder. n Scratch.app n Scratch.image n License.txt Instructions for Executing Your Application from a CD-ROM Once you have burned a CD-ROM for your Scratch application, you need to tell your friends how to execute it, which can be done by double-clicking on Screatch.exe (Windows) or Scratch.app (Mac OS X), which will start the Scratch IDE, after which your application can be accessed by clicking on the IDE's Open button. Alternatively, for Windows users, you might want to consider adding a batch file for each application that you added to the CD-ROM that when executed will run one of your Scratch applications. You can do this by opening your preferred text editor (such as Notepad) and keying in a single statement using the following syntax. Scratch.exe Scratch.image ScratchProject.sb Here, Scratch.exe is the name of the Scratch executable that starts Scratch. Scratch.image is a required Scratch system file, and ScratchProject.sb represents the name of a Scratch application that you have added to the CD-ROM. Note that the .sb file extension has been included. Once you have typed in this statement, save the text file with a filename that ends with a .bat file extension (MrWiggly.bat, HelloWorld.bat, etc.). When a batch file is added to the CD-ROM along with all of the files already listed, your friends can start your Scratch application by double-clicking on it. Once double-clicked, the batch file will open Scratch and load your Scratch application project into it, making it ready for execution.

Summary

This chapter walked you through the development of your second Scratch project. In learning how to create Mr. Wiggly's Dance, you learned the fundamental steps involved in creating and executing Scratch applications. This included learning how to change stage backgrounds and work with sprites. Although detailed instruction on how to work with different code blocks and sounds is not covered until later chapters, you received a quick overview of how to work with a number of control, motion, looks, and sound blocks, and you learned how to import audio files and sprites into your Scratch applications.

CHAPTER SIX

Moving Things Around

This chapter is the first of eight chapters designed to teach you how to work with all of the code blocks that make up the Scratch programming language. This chapter's focus is on demonstrating how to work with motion code blocks. Using these blocks, you will be able to create Scratch applications that can move sprites around the stage, rotate sprites, point them in different directions, change sprite location, detect collisions with the edge of the stage, and report on a sprite's direction and coordinates. This chapter also introduces you to Scratch cards as a means for learning how to perform different types of tasks. You will also learn how to create a new virtual fish tank application. The major topics covered in this chapter include:

Learning how to move and rotate sprites

Learning how to change sprite direction and location

Learning how to change sprite location and to detect collisions with the edge of the stage

Learning how to retrieve and report information about a sprite's coordinates and direction

Working with Motion Code Blocks To move sprites around the stage when your Scratch applications execute, you need to learn how to work with motion code blocks. As previously stated, motion blocks control sprite placement, direction, rotation, and movement. In total, Scratch provides access to 16 different motion blocks, which you can work with by clicking on the Motion button located at the top of the blocks palette and then dragging and dropping motion blocks onto the scripts area, where you can configure them and use them in creating scripts. If you look closely at the various motion code blocks, you will notice that Scratch organizes them into six subgroupings, each of which is separated by a blank space in the blocks palette. These sub groupings include: n Motion blocks that move and rotate sprites n Motion blocks that point sprites in different directions or towards different objects n Motion blocks that change a sprite's location and control whether a sprite jumps to its new location or glides to it n Motion blocks that change a sprite location by setting or modifying the value of its X-axis and Y-axis coordinates n A motion block that controls a sprite's movement when it touches the edges of the stage n Motion blocks that report on a sprite's position and direction Examples of how to work with the motion code blocks in each of these subgroups are provided throughout the rest of this chapter.

Moving and Rotating Sprites Scratch provides access to three motion blocks that move sprites and rotate them on their axis. These code blocks are shown in Figure 5.1. The first of these blocks allows you to specify the number of steps that a sprite should be moved on the stage (in whatever direction the sprite is currently pointing). By default, the code block specifies a value of 10. However, you may

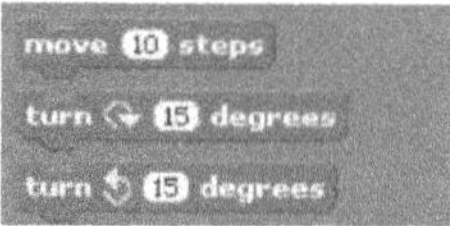

Figure 5.1
These control blocks are designed to give you control over the relative movement and rotation of sprites.

change this value to suit your needs. You can even enter a negative value to move the sprite in the opposite direction that it is pointing.

In addition, you can drag and drop any reporter block you want into this code block's entry field when specifying a value. The next two code blocks provide the ability to rotate a sprite on its axis, clockwise and counterclockwise, as indicated by the direction of the arrow displayed on the blocks.

The following sample script demonstrates how to use the first two blocks to move a sprite around the stage in a clockwise manner.

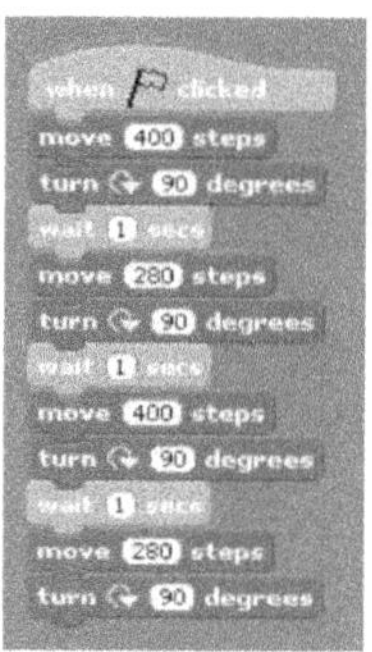

This script executes whenever the green flag button is clicked. Once this event has occurred, four pairs of motion code blocks are executed at one-second intervals. This application uses the default cat sprite that is supplied as part of every new Scratch project. To create and test your own copy of the application, create a new Scratch application, click on the thumbnail of the cat sprite, drag it to the upper-left corner of the stage, and shrink it to about 50% of its normal size and then assemble the script.

The first two motion blocks in the script move the sprite 400 steps. Since the cat, by default, is pointed 90 degrees to the left, this will move the sprite from the upper-left corner of the stage to the upper-right corner of the stage. The next pair of motion blocks moves the sprite down to the bottom-right corner of the stage. The third pair of motion blocks moves the sprite to the bottom-left corner of the stage, and the last pair of motion blocks moves it back to the upper-left corner of the stage.

If you want, you can modify the script to move the sprite around the stage in a counterclockwise direction by modifying it, as demonstrated here:

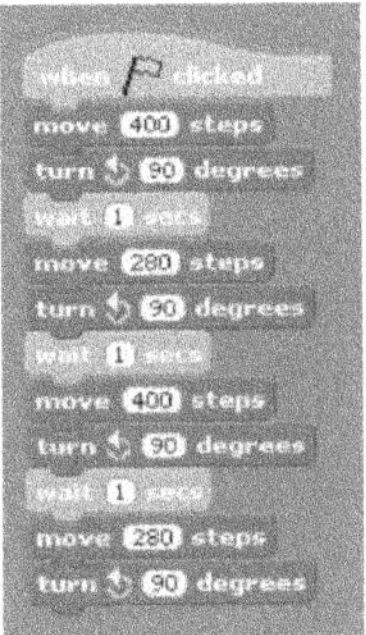

Setting Sprite Direction

Scratch provides access to two motion blocks that can be used to point a sprite in a specified direction or to point a sprite towards the mouse-pointer or a specified sprite. These code blocks are shown in Figure 5.3.

The first of these blocks allows you to point a sprite in a particular direction as specified by the assignment of a numeric value representing the number of degrees that the sprite should be turned. You can either select a value of 0 = up, 90 = right, −90 = left, or 180 = down from the block's drop-down list or type in an integer value in the range of 0 to 360. For example, the following script demonstrates how to rotate a sprite 360 degrees, 90 degrees at a time at one-second intervals.

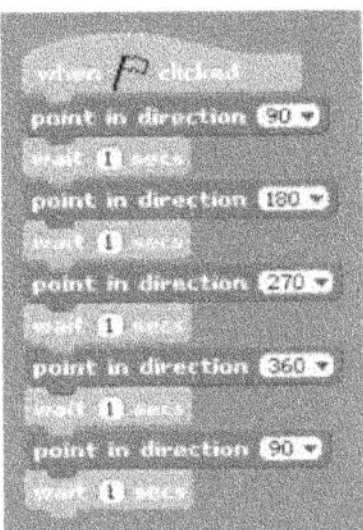

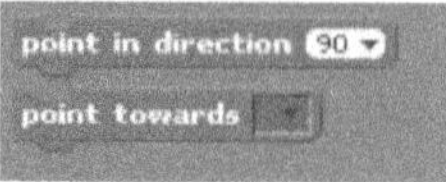

Figure 5.3
These code blocks can be used to point a sprite towards a specified direction or object.

Figure 5.4
An example of the four possible directions that the point in direction code block can point a sprite.

Figure 5.5
The cat rotates as necessary to continue facing the mouse-pointer.

This example uses the default cat sprite. Figure 5.4 shows an example of the four directions that the sprite turns when the script is executed. Note that for this example to work, you must click on the Can Rotate button in the sprite info area (allowing the sprite to rotate over a range of 360 degrees).

The second motion block shown in Figure 5.5 lets you point a sprite towards either the mouse-pointer or another sprite, as demonstrated in the following script.

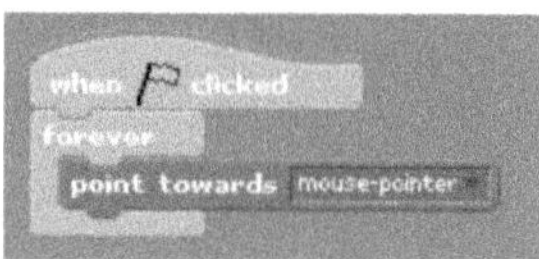

In this example, the sprite is continuously repositioned so that is points towards the mouse-pointer. Therefore, whenever the mouse-pointer is moved around the stage, the image of the cat follows, as demonstrated in Figure 5.5.

Note

In order for the sprite shown in Figure 5.5 to continuously reposition itself, the motion block must be embedded within a control block that sets up a loop, repeatedly executing the motion block, allowing it to react every time the mouse-pointer is moved.

Repositioning a Sprite

Scratch provides access to three motion blocks that move a sprite to a specified coordination location on the stage, move a sprite to the location currently occupied by the mouse-pointer or another sprite, or move a sprite to a specified coordination position over a specified number of seconds. These code blocks are shown in Figure 5.6.

The first of these three motion blocks allows you to reposition a sprite to any location on the stage by specifying X-axis and Y-axis coordinates for the sprite. For example, the following script demonstrates how to reposition a sprite in the middle of the stage, pointing it in a 90-degree direction.

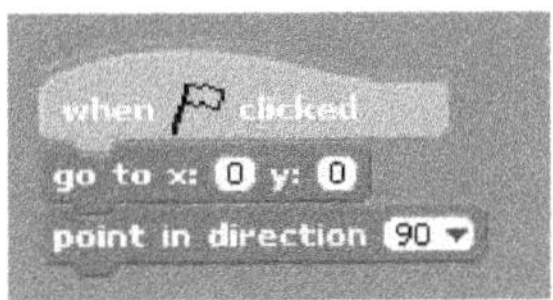

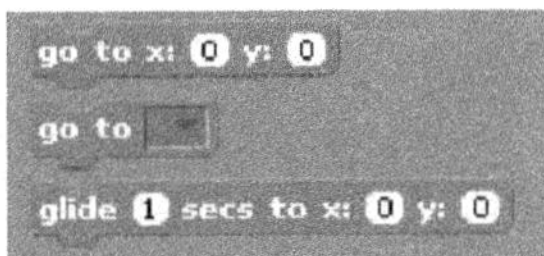

Figure 5.6
These code blocks can be used to move a sprite to a specific location.

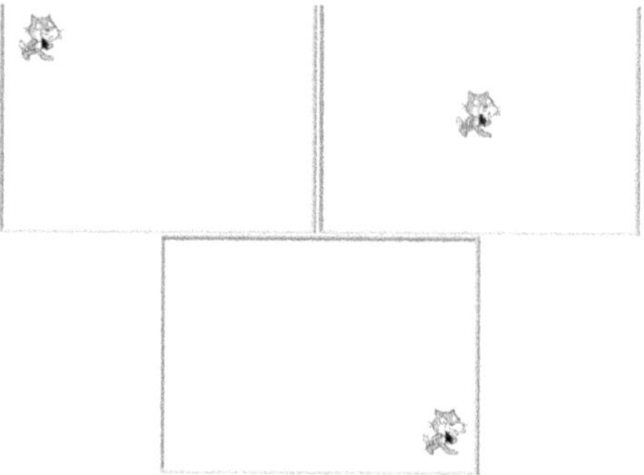

Figure 5.7
As this figure demonstrates, the sprite automatically moves around the stage, following the mouse-pointer.

The following script demonstrates how to move a sprite to the location on the stage currently occupied by the mouse-pointer.

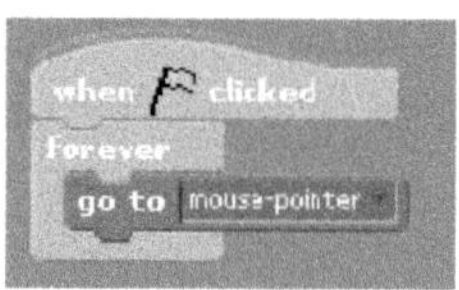

Figure 5.7 shows an example of the output that is generated when this script is run. If you look closely, you will see that in each of the three examples, the cat sprite remains positioned directly under the mouse-pointer no matter where it is moved on the stage.

This next script demonstrates how to reposition a sprite to a specific location on the stage. Instead of simply making the sprite appear at a specified location, as demonstrated in the previous two examples, this script repositions the sprite by moving or gliding to its new position in a smooth motion.

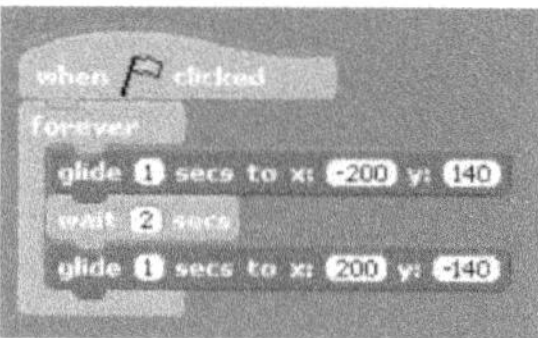

Changing Sprite Coordinates

Scratch provides four motion blocks that modify the location of a sprite on the stage either by assigning it new coordinates or by changing the sprite's coordinates by incrementing or decrementing their values. These code blocks are shown in Figure 5.8.

The following script demonstrates how to move a sprite across the stage in a series of eight steps. When first started, the script moves the sprite to the left-hand side of the stage, and then, using a loop, the sprite is moved by incrementing the value assigned to the X-axis coordinate by 50 and its Y-axis coordinate by −10 each time the loop repeats itself. As a result, the sprite is repeatedly repositioned and thus moved across the stage (in a descending angle over a period of eight seconds).

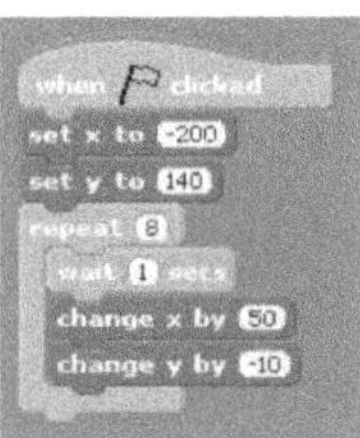

Bouncing Sprites Around the Stage

As a sprite is moved around the stage, it may eventually come into contact with one of the edges of the stage. Using the motion block shown next, you can instruct Scratch to bounce the sprite off of the edge of the stage.

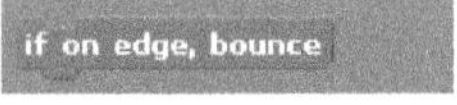

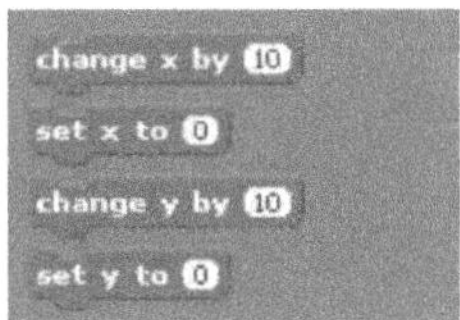

Figure 5.8
These code blocks provide the ability to modify a sprite's location by changing its coordinates.

The following script demonstrates how to use this code block to bounce a sprite around the stage:

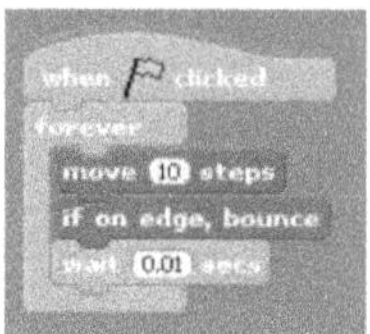

This script reverses the direction that a sprite is traveling whenever it collides with the edge of the stage. If you were to add this script to the cat sprite in a new application, the cat would move across the stage from side to side until you halted the application's execution.

Keeping Track of Sprite Coordinates and Direction

Scratch provides three motion (reporter) blocks that can be used to retrieve and display information regarding the value of the sprite's X- and Y-coordinates as well as the sprite's direction. These code blocks are shown in Figure 5.9.

Note

Scratch's stage coordinate system allows for a coordinate range of -240 to 240 on its X-axis and a coordinate range of 180 to -180 on its Y-axis.

To set up an example that demonstrates how to work with these reporter blocks, create a new Scratch application and add the following script to the default cat sprite.

When executed, this script will move the cat sprite around the stage to wherever the mouse-pointer is located, bouncing it off the edge of the stage when necessary. After adding the script, select each of the reporter blocks by clicking on

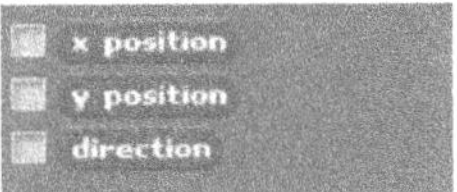

Figure 5.9
These code blocks provide the ability to retrieve and display a sprite's coordinates and direction.

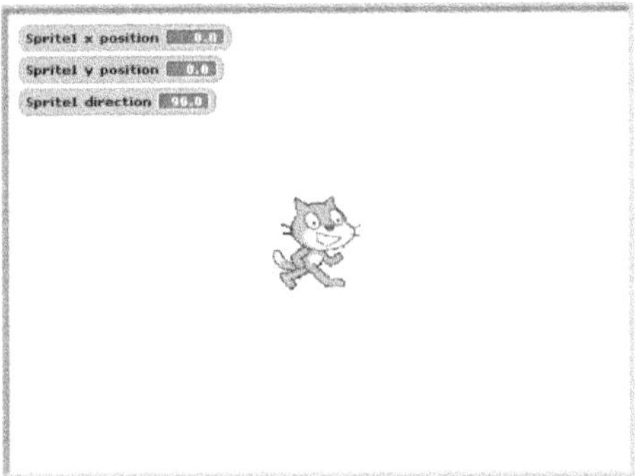

Figure 5.10
Displaying a sprite's coordinates and direction.

the check box just to the left of each block in the blocks palette. Once you have done this, three monitors should be visible on the stage, as demonstrated in Figure 5.10.

Once you have set up the application's monitors, run the application, move the mouse-pointer around the stage, and keep an eye on the values reported by the monitors.

Taking Advantage of Scratch Cards

One resource available to Scratch programmers is Scratch cards. *Scratch cards* are PDF files that you can print, cut out, glue together, and then use as a quick reference for performing certain tasks. You can download Scratch cards for free at http://scratch.wik.is/Support/Scratch_Cards, as shown in Figure 5.11.

The front of each Scratch card identifies the type of task that the card is designed to show you how to perform, and the back of the card provides detailed

Figure 5.11
Scratch cards serve as quick reference for performing specific types of tasks.

instruction on how to perform the task. As of the writing of this book, a dozen Scratch cards were available. The PDF file for each of these Scratch cards is descriptively named to identify the task that the card teaches you to perform. The list of available Scratch cards includes:

- Change Color
- Move to a Beat
- Key Moves
- Say Something
- Glide
- Follow the Mouse
- Dance Twist

- Interactive Whirl

- Animate It

- Moving Animation

- Surprise Button

- Keep Score

Figure 5.12 shows what the PDF file for the Key Moves Scratch card looks like. As you can see, the left-hand side of the Scratch card demonstrates the movement of

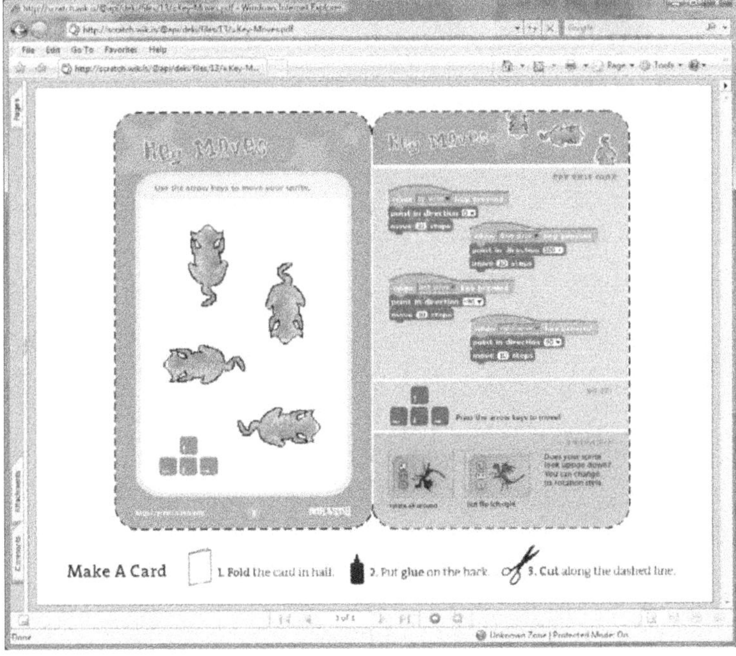

Figure 5.12
The Key Moves Scratch card demonstrates how to move a sprite around the stage using the keyboard arrow keys.

the sprite, and the right-hand side of the card provides an example of the code blocks needed to move the sprite in each of the four demonstrated directions. In addition, each Scratch card includes an extra tip that helps you further enhance the task being performed.

Tip

There are five Scratch cards that provide information specific to moving sprites around the stage. These Scratch cards are briefly described here:

- **Key Moves.** Demonstrates how to move a sprite around the stage using keyboard keys.

- **Move to a Beat.** Demonstrates how to create an animated dance sequence that moves to a drum beat.

- **Moving Animation.** Demonstrates how to animate the movements of a sprite using an alternative series of costumes.

- **Glide.** Demonstrates how to move a sprite around the stage from one point to another in a smooth motion.

- **Follow the Mouse.** Demonstrates how to script the movement of a sprite so that it follows the movement of the mouse-pointer on the stage.

Creating the Virtual Scratch Fish Tank

The rest of this chapter is dedicated to leading you through the development of a virtual fish tank application. In this Scratch application, five sprites, representing a range of colorful fish and a small octopus, busily swim around the fish tank, represented by a suitable background, as demonstrated in Figure 5.13.

This application will be created by following a series of steps, as outlined here:

1. Creating a new Scratch application project.

2. Adding a stage background.

3. Adding and removing sprites to and from the project.

4. Importing a sound file into the application.

5. Adding the programming logic required to play a background sound effect.

6. Adding the programming logic required to animate fish tank activity.

7. Saving and executing your work.

Figure 5.13
An example of the virtual fish tank application in action.

Step 1: Creating a New Scratch Project

The first step in creating this Scratch project is to start Scratch, thereby auto-matically creating a new Scratch application project. Alternatively, if you already have Scratch up and running, you can create a new project by clicking on the New button located on the Scratch menu bar.

Step 2: Adding a Background to the Stage

Once you have a new application project ready to go, let's begin by adding a suitable background to the stage that will give the virtual fish tank an appropriate look and feel. To set this up, click on the blank thumbnail representing the stage in the sprite list and then click on the Backgrounds tab located at the top of the scripts area. Next, click on the Import button, displaying the Import Background window. Double-click on the Nature folder, scroll down and select the underwater graphic, and then click on the OK button. Once the new background has been added, go ahead and remove the blank stage background from the application.

Step 3: Adding and Removing Sprites

The next step in the development of the virtual fish tank application is to add sprites to the application representing different marine life. Before doing this, remove the cat sprite from the application, since it is not needed. To do so,

Table 5.1 Sprite Rotational Buttons

Sprite Filename	Sprite Application Name
fish2	Purple
fish3	Yellow
fish4	Spotted
octopus1-a	Squid

right-click on its thumbnail in the sprites list and select Delete from the popup menu that appears. Once you have removed the cat sprite, it is time to add new sprites needed by the application.

In total, you need to add five new sprites. Four of the sprites will represent different fish, and the fifth sprite will represent a small octopus. To add the octopus sprite, click on the Choose Sprite from File button located in the middle of the new sprite button controls. This will open the New Sprite window. Double-click on the Animals folder, scroll down and select the fish1-a sprite, and then click on the OK button. Next, click on the sprite's thumbnail in the sprites area and then change the name assigned to the sprite to Blue.

Using the same set of steps described above, add the following list of sprites to the application project, renaming each sprite as indicated in Table 5.1.

Once you have added all five sprites, move the sprites to random locations on the stage. Next, change the direction in which each sprite moves by selecting each sprite and then changing it in the sprite info area by repositioning the direction of the blue line displayed on the image of the sprite.

Tip

To make the virtual fish tank more interesting, set the fish and the octopus up so that each moves in a different direction and angle.

Step 4: Adding a Suitable Audio File to the Stage

Now that the application's background and sprites have been added, it is time to add an audio file that when played will give the virtual fish tank a realistic feeling. Specifically, we'll add an audio file that when played makes bubble sounds. To accomplish this task, click on the thumbnail representing the stage in the sprite list and then click on the Sounds tab in the scripts area. Next, click on the Import button to display the Import Sound window. Next, double-click on the Effects folder and then select the Bubble audio file and click on OK.

Tip

> To help keep your Scratch application as small as possible, remove the default pop audio file from the background.

Step 5: Playing the Audio File

Now it is time to add the programming logic needed to make your new application run. In total you will need to add six scripts to the project, one for the stage and one for each of the application's five sprites.

The script to be added to the stage will be responsible for playing the background sound effect that makes the virtual fish tank sound like a real fish tank. To create it, click on the stage thumbnail located in the sprites area and then select the Scripts tab located at the top of the scripts area. Next, add and configure the following code blocks exactly as shown here:

This script consists of a hat block that will execute whenever the green flag button is pressed. When this occurs, a loop is set up that repeatedly executes two blocks. The first code block is a sound block that plays the audio file you previously added to the stage. The second code block pauses script execution for four seconds to give Scratch time to finish playing the audio file, before allowing the loop to repeat and play it again.

Step 6: Animating the Swimming of the Fish

With the programming logic required to provide the application's background sound effect now in place, it is time to write the scripts that will animate the movement of the fish and octopus. To set this up, you need to add a small script to each of the sprites that provides the programming logic required to control the movement of the sprites as they move (or swim) around the fish tank.

Scripting the Movement of the Blue Fish

Let's begin by automating the movement of the sprite name Blue. Do so by clicking on the sprite's thumbnail and then creating the following script for it:

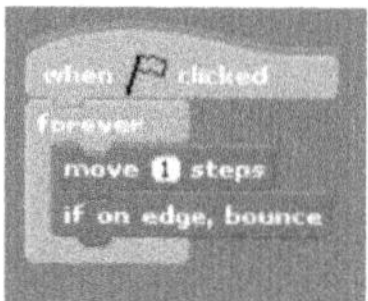

As you can see, this script is set up to begin executing the moment the user clicks on the green flag button. It contains a control block that sets up a loop that repeats the execution of two embedded motion blocks. The first motion block moves the sprite in its current direction every time the loop repeats. The second motion block tells Scratch to bounce the sprite off of the edge of the stage when reached. As a result, the sprite (blue fish) will appear to swim around the fish tank from side to side, and depending on whether you have adjusted its direction as instructed at the end of Step 3, it will move up and down as well.

Scripting the Movement of the Purple Fish

Next, let's create a script that controls the movement of the purple fish. Rather than build this script from scratch, let's take a shortcut. With the script for the blue fish currently displayed on the scripts area, drag and drop the script onto the thumbnail representing the purple sprite in the sprites list. This adds an exact copy of the script to the purple sprite, which you can then view and modify by clicking on the purple sprite's thumbnail.

To make things interesting, modify the number of steps that the purple sprite is moved from 1 to 2, as shown here:

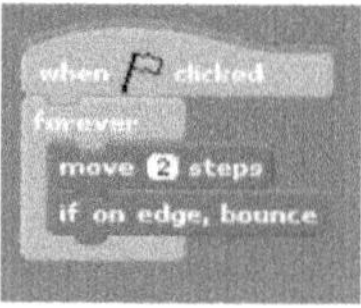

Other than moving the purple fish at a little faster pace than the blue fish, the programming logic that controls both fish is identical. In fact, the programming for all of the remaining fish and the octopus is identical, except for variances in the number of steps the sprites are moved.

Scripting the Movement of the Yellow Fish

Using drag and drop, add a copy of the purple sprite's script to the yellow sprite and then modify it as shown here:

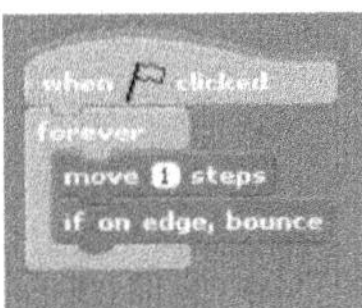

As you can see, the yellow sprite has been configured to move at the same pace as the blue sprite.

Scripting the Movement of the Spotted Fish

Once again, using drag and drop, add a copy of the yellow sprite's script to the spotted sprite and then modify it as shown here:

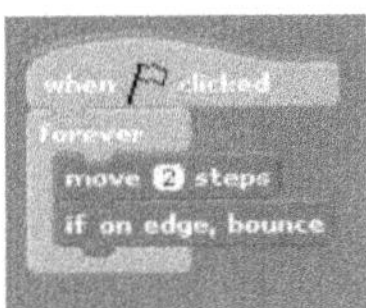

This time the sprite has been configured so that it moves two steps at a time.

Scripting the Movement of the Octopus

Last but not least, drag and drop the script for the spotted sprite onto the sprite representing the octopus and then modify it as shown here:

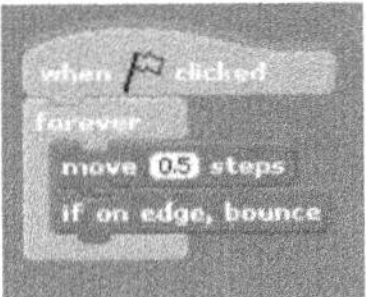

As you can see, this sprite has been configured to move slower than any of the other sprites, at just a half step at a time.

Step 7: Saving and Executing Your New Scratch Application

At this point your copy of the virtual fish tank application should be complete and should look like the example shown in Figure 5.14.

If you have not done so yet, save your new application and then run it to see how it looks. To save your application, click on the Save button located on the Scratch menu bar. This will display the Save Project window, allowing you to specify the name of the application, the location where you want to store it, your name, and comments documenting the application and its purpose.

Figure 5.14
The completed application consists of a background, five sprites, and six scripts.

Once you have saved your application, go ahead and run it. Since all of the scripts in the application are configured to execute when the green flag button is pressed, all you have to do is to click on the green flag button and then sit back and relax as you watch and listen to your virtual fish tank.

Summary

This chapter taught you how to work with all 16 motion code blocks. You learned how to move and rotate sprites, point sprites in different directions or towards different objects, and change a sprite's location. You also learned how to control whether a sprite jumps to its new location or glides to it, how to change a sprite's location by setting or modifying the value of its X-axis and Y-axis coordinates, how to control a sprite's movement when it makes contact with the edge of the stage, and how to report on a sprite's position and direction. You also learned how to work with Scratch cards and create a virtual fish tank application.

CHAPTER SEVEN

Doing Some Math with Logic

Scratch provides robust support for performing mathematical calculations. This gives you the ability to develop applications that can manipulate numeric data in a variety of ways. Scratch provides this support through numbers code blocks. Numbers code blocks are reporter blocks and therefore can only be used in conjunction with stack code blocks. This chapter will provide a thorough review of each of these code blocks and will also show you how to create a new Scratch application, the Number Guessing game.

The major topics covered in this chapter include:

- Learning how to add, subtract, multiply, and divide programmatically
- Learning how to generate random numbers using any range you specify
- Instruction on how to perform different types of numeric comparisons
- Learning how to perform a number of built-in mathematical operations

Addition, Subtraction, Multiplication, and Division

Like all modern programming languages, Scratch provides programmers with the ability to add, subtract, multiply, and divide numeric data. This capability is offered through the code blocks shown in Figure 8.1.

Figure 8.1
These code blocks provide Scratch programmers with the ability to perform arithmetic calculations.

The use of these code blocks is quite intuitive, with each code block clearly identifying its usage. These code blocks can be embedded within any Scratch code block that accepts numeric input. For example, the following script demonstrates how to use these code blocks to modify the value assigned to a variable named Count.

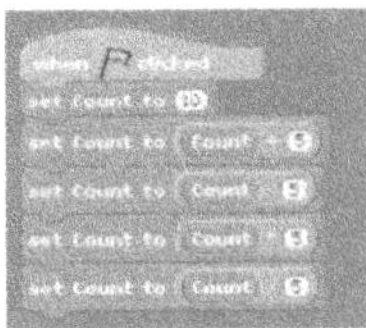

Here, the script begins by assigning an initial value of 10 to Count. Next, four sets of code blocks are executed. Each set consists of one stack block and two reporter blocks. The first set of statements sets the value of Count equal to the value currently assigned to Count plus 5, making Count equal to 15. The second set of code blocks sets Count equal to the value currently assigned to Count minus 5, making Count equal to 10. The third set of code blocks sets Count equal to the current value of Count times 5, making Count equal to 50. Lastly, the last set of code blocks changes the value of Count to 10 by dividing its current value by 5.

Understanding the Mathematical Order of Precedence

As is the case with all programming languages, Scratch allows you to string together different combinations of numbers code blocks in order to create more complicated numeric calculations. For example, take a look at the following script.

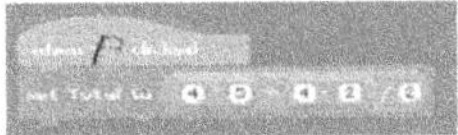

Here, a small script has been created that evaluates a numeric expression and assigns the result to a variable named Total. This equation was created by embedding a series of numbers code blocks within one another. Specifically, the

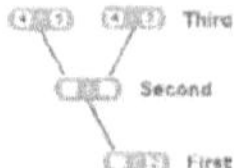

Figure 8.2
Creating complex formulas by assembling different combinations of code blocks.

equation was created by embedding the code blocks shown in Figure 8.2 into one another.

As shown in Figure 8.2, the equation was assembled by embedding the division code block into a variable block. Next, the addition code block was embedded within the left-hand side of the division code block. Finally, a multiplication code block and a subtraction code block are embedded within the input fields of the addition code block.

Like all programming languages, Scratch evaluates the components of mathematical expressions by following a specific order, referred to as the *order of precedence*. Specifically, Scratch evaluates an expression using a top-down approach. When applied to the example shown in Figures 8.2, Scratch evaluates it as follows:

1. First, it calculates the value of the two top code blocks. Therefore, 4 is multiplied by 5, yielding a value of 20, and 2 is subtracted from 4, yielding a value of 2. At this stage, the expression has been evaluated as shown here.

   20 + 2 / 2

2. Next, the expression located in the second level code bock (the addition block) is evaluated. Therefore, 20 is added to 2, yielding a value of 22. At this stage, the expression has been evaluated as shown here.

   22 / 2

3. Finally, the lowest level code block is evaluated, dividing 22 by 2 and resulting in a final value of 11.

Generating a Random Number

Some applications, such as computer games, require an element of randomness or chance. For example, a game that needs to simulate the rolling of dice needs to be able to create a pair of random numbers in the range of 1 to 6. Scratch provides the capability through the code block shown in Figure 8.3.

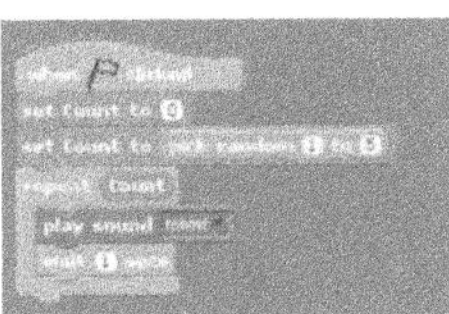

Figure 8.3
By default, this code block is configured to generate a number in the range of 1 to 10.

This code block provides a means of generating random integer (whole) numbers using any specified range of numbers. The default range is 1 to 10, but you may change the input fields to suit your needs. If needed, you can generate negative numbers. In addition to hard coding a numeric range into the control, you can substitute variable blocks by dragging and dropping them into either or both of this code block's input fields.

To develop an understanding of how this code block works, look at the following example:

Here, a script has been created that begins by assigning a variable named Count a starting value of 0. Next, the variable's value is changed by assigning it a randomly selected value in the range of 1 to 5. A loop is then set up to repeat the execution of two embedded code blocks. The loop is designed to repeat a specified number of times and is set up by default to execute 10 times. However, by dragging and dropping an instance of the Count variable block into the loop's input field, the number of times that the loop executes is randomly determined, depending on the randomly assigned value of Count.

Note

> Each time the loop executes, it plays an audio file that sounds like a cat meowing. In order to give the audio file time to finish playing, a control block was added to pause script execution for one second. To see this script in action, create a new Scratch application and add the script to the default Cat sprite.

Comparison Operations

In order to work with numbers, you often need to mathematically manipulate them as demonstrated in the previous section. Doing so will ultimately leave you with a result. Typically, you will want to do something with this result once it has

Figure 8.4
These code blocks provide the ability to compare any two numeric values.

been calculated. For a simple application, all you may need to do is display its value. However, more often than not, you are going to end up using it to guide the execution of your application in some manner. For example, suppose you want to create a number guessing game that automatically generates a random number and then challenges the player to try to guess it. Once the random number is generated and stored in a variable, the player needs to be prompted to try to guess it (perhaps by clicking on one of 10 buttons with numbers printed on them). Once the player's guess is captured, the application needs to compare the player's guess against the value of the variable that stores the game's random number to determine whether the player's guess is correct. To facilitate this type of comparison operation, Scratch provides access to the three code blocks shown in Figure 8.4.

The first and last code blocks shown in Figure 8.4 allow you to compare one value against a range of values. The first code block checks to see if the numeric value specified in its first input field is less than the value specified in its second input field. The third code block does the opposite, checking to see if the numeric value specified in its first input field is greater than the value specified in its second input field. The middle code block is used to determine if two values are equal.

To develop a better understanding of how to work with each of these three code blocks, let's look at a few examples. In the first example, shown below, a script has been created that executes whenever the green flag button is clicked. When this happens, the value Count is set equal to 10. Next, a numbers block is embedded within a control block to set up a conditional test that evaluates the value assigned to Count and to execute the code block embedded within the control block in the event that the tested condition (Count equals 10) is true. Since this is the case, a text string of Hello! is displayed in a speech bubble.

Note

To prove that the embedded numbers code block is working as it is supposed to, you could change the value assigned to Count to something other than 10 and run the example again. Since the value assigned to Count no longer equals 10, the tested condition would evaluate as false, and the text message would not display.

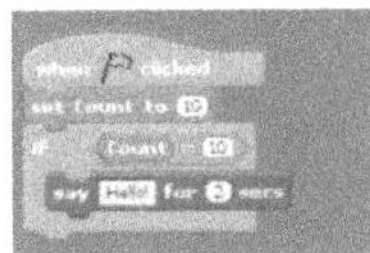

In this next example, the numbers code block that tests for greater than conditions is used. Again, a script has been set up to execute whenever the green flag button is clicked. The value assigned to Count is then set to 1, and a control block is used to set up a loop that runs forever (until you provide a means for stopping its execution). A number of code blocks are embedded within the loop. The first block plays an audio file, and the second block pauses script execution for one second to allow Scratch time to finish playing the file. Another control block is then used to set up a conditional test that evaluates the value assigned to Count to see if it is greater than 2, and if it is, another control block is used to terminate the script's execution. If the value assigned to Count is not greater than 2, then the last code block located at the bottom of the loop is executed, incrementing the value of Count by 1. The loop then repeats and executes again.

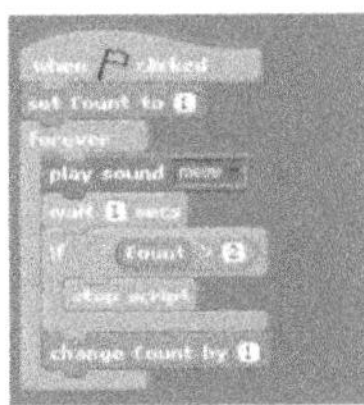

The first time the loop runs, the value assigned to Count is 1. The loop must iterate two times before the value of Count is set to 3, resulting in the termination of the script's execution. Because of this, the audio file will play three times.

In this final example, shown next, the numbers code block that tests for less than conditions is used. Like the last two examples, this script is set up to execute whenever the green flag button is clicked. When this happens, the value of Count is set to 1. Next, a loop is set up that repeatedly executes as long as the value of Count is less than 15. Each time this test evaluates as true, three embedded code blocks are executed. The first code block moves the sprite 25 steps. The next code block increments the value assigned to Count by 1, and the last code block pauses script execution for one second.

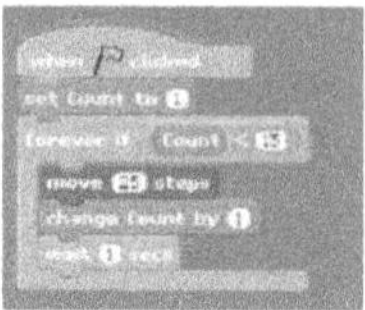

The way this script is written, its loop will execute 14 times and will stop executing when the value of Count finally reaches 15.

Trick

While Scratch only supplies you with three code blocks for performing conditional tests (equality, greater than, and less than), most programming languages support three additional types of conditional tests, allowing you to perform the following comparison operations:

- Greater than or equal to

- Less than or equal to

- Not equal to

Although Scratch does not provide equivalent code blocks, you can easily set up equivalent comparison tests by combining the three code blocks just discussed with Scratch's logical comparison code blocks, as shown in Figure 8.5.

The first combination of code blocks shown in Figure 8.5 creates a test that determines if the value assigned to a variable named Total is less than or equal to 10. This example is made up of five code blocks—two variable blocks, two numbers code blocks used to perform less than and equality comparisons, and another numbers block, which is used to tie everything together. The second combination of code blocks shown in Figure 8.5 is very similar and is designed to create a test that checks to see if the value assigned to Total is greater than or equal to 5. The last example is made up of three code blocks and is used to evaluate the values assigned to Total to determine to see if it is not equal to 3. You will learn more about code blocks that support logical comparisons in the next section.

Figure 8.5
Creating customized logical comparisons.

Performing Logical Comparisons

In addition to code blocks designed to perform mathematical and comparison operations, Scratch also provides access to three code blocks that support logical comparison operations. These code blocks are shown in Figure 8.6.

The first code block is used to test two different sets of values to determine if both are true. The second code block is used to test two different sets of values to determine if at least one is true. And the last code block lets you evaluate two values to determine if the tested condition is false (not true).

To help you better understand how to work with all three of these code blocks, let's review a few examples. The first example, shown next, is a script that executes whenever the green flag button is clicked. When this occurs, the value assigned to the variable Count is set to 50. Next, a control code block is used to analyze the value assigned to Count. If the value of Count is less than 100 and also greater than 10, then the end statement embedded within the control block is executed. However, if both tested conditions evaluate as false, the embedded code block is not executed.

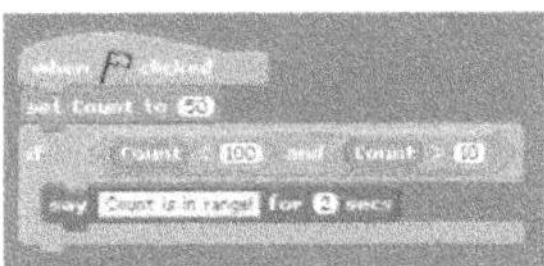

Note

Scratch is very flexible in its support for numbers blocks. For example, if you prefer, you could swap the order in which the two embedded numbers blocks occur (e.g., checking to see that Count is greater than 10 before checking to make sure that Count is also less than 100), and the results would be the same.

This next example is very similar to the previous example, except that instead of ensuring that both tested conditions evaluate as being true, the script has been

Figure 8.6
Using these code blocks, you can perform more complex comparison operations.

modified so that only one of the tested conditions has to be evaluated as true in order for the embedded code block to be executed.

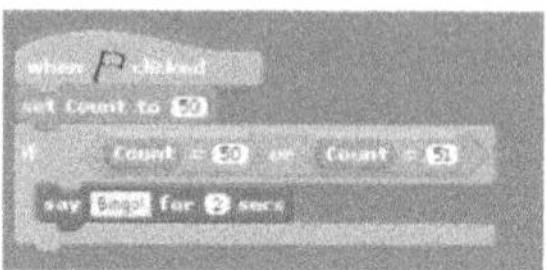

This final example shows a script that performs a negative test, checking to see if two values are not equal instead of checking to see if they are equal. As a result, if the value assigned to Count is not equal to 50, which it is not, the code block embedded within the control block is executed.

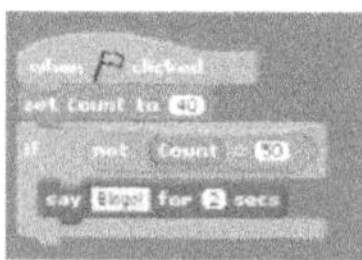

Rounding Numbers and Retrieving Remainders

The next set of numbers code blocks, shown in Figure 8.7, provides the ability to retrieve the remainder portion of any division operation and lets you round any decimal number to the nearest whole number.

The first code block shown in Figure 8.7 returns the remainder portion of a division operation, also referred to as a modulus, as demonstrated in the following example, which divides 10 by 3 and then assigns the modulus (a value of 1) to a variable named Remainder.

Figure 8.7
These code blocks retrieve remainders and round numbers.

The second code block shown in Figure 8.7 returns the rounded value for a specified numeric value, rounded to the nearest whole number, as demonstrated in the following examples, which return values of 4 and 5, respectively.

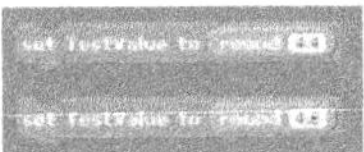

Working with Built-in Mathematical Functions

In addition to all of the mathematical operations that you can put together using the numbers code blocks previously discussed in this chapter, Scratch provides one additional multi purpose code block, as shown in Figure 8.8.

This code block is designed to perform any of 12 different mathematical functions, which can be selected from the code block's drop-down list. The functions that this code block can perform are outlined in the following list:

- **abs.** Returns the absolute, non-negative value of a number.

- **sqrt.** Returns the square root of a number.

- **sin.** Returns a value representing the sine of an angle.

- **cos.** Returns a value representing the cosine of an angle.

- **tan.** Returns a value representing the tangent of an angle.

- **asin.** Returns the arc sine for the specified numeric value.

- **acos.** Returns the arc cosine for the specified numeric value.

- **atan.** Returns the arc tangent for the specific numeric value.

- **ln.** Returns the inverse of the natural exponent of a specified value (i.e., the opposite of e^).

- **log.** Returns the natural log of a number.

Figure 8.8
This code block can assist you in setting up extremely complex calculations.

- **e^**. Returns the natural exponent of a specified value.

- **10^**. Returns the value of a number raised to the 10th power.

These code blocks can be real time savers when developing applications that require the use of any of the mathematical functions supported by the code block, saving you the trouble of implementing the underlying programming logic yourself to retrieve similar results. As a result, not only will you spend less time working on the development of your application, but the programming logic that you have to develop will be simplified and easier to maintain, since this code block can do most of the heavy lifting for you.

To specify which function you want to work with, all you have to do is select it from the code block's drop-down list. For example, the following examples demonstrate the use of two different functions provided by this code block:

This example consists of two sets of code blocks. The first set of code blocks returns the absolute value of –4.4, which is 4.4, and assigns that value to a variable named Result. The second set of blocks returns the square root of 9, which is 3, and assigns that value to a variable named Result.

Developing the Number Guessing Game Quiz Project

The remainder of this chapter is focused on the development of your next Scratch application, the Number Guessing game. This application will make use of numbers code blocks to generate random numbers for the player to guess and to compare the player's guesses against the game's randomly generated number.

In total, the application is made up of a background, 11 sprites, and 12 scripts. When run, the game will challenge the player to guess a randomly generated number in the range of 0 to 9 in as few guesses as possible. Figure 8.9 shows an example of how the game looks when first started.

To enter a guess, the player must click on one of the button sprites located at the bottom of the stage. The cat provides immediate feedback after each guess, as demonstrated in Figure 8.10.

Figure 8.9
The Number Guessing game is moderated by the Cat sprite.

Figure 8.10
The cat lets the player know when guesses are too high or too low.

Figure 8.11
The player guessed the secret number in five guesses.

Figure 8.11 shows how the game looks once the player finally manages to guess the game's secret random number.

The game automatically generates a new random number at the end of each game, in order to ready the game to be played again. The development of this application project will be created by following a series of steps, as outlined here:

1. Creating a new Scratch application project.

2. Adding a background to the stage.

3. Adding and removing sprites.

4. Adding variables needed by the application.

5. Adding an audio file to the application.

6. Adding scripts to each button to collect player guesses.

7. Adding the programming logic required to process player guesses.

8. Saving and executing your work.

Step 1: Creating a New Scratch Project

The first step in the development of the Number Guessing game is to create a new Scratch application project. To do so, start Scratch, automatically creating a new Scratch project or, if Scratch is already running, click on the New button located on the Scratch menu bar.

Step 2: Adding a Stage Background

The next step in the development of the Number Guessing game is to add a background to the stage. To do so, click on the blank stage thumbnail located in the sprite list and then change its background by clicking on the Backgrounds tab located at the top of the scripts area. Next, click on the Import button and when the Import Background window opens, click on the Outdoors folder. Then select the brick-wall1 thumbnail and click on the OK button. Since the application only needs one background, remove the default blank background, named background1, from your project by clicking on the Delete This Costume button.

Step 3: Adding and Removing Sprites

The Number Guessing game is comprised of the default Cat sprite plus 10 button sprites and a variable monitor, as shown in Figure 8.12.

Figure 8.12
An overview of the different parts of the Number Guessing game.

To add the first of the sprites representing the 10 input buttons, click on the Choose New Sprite from File button to open the New Sprite window. Drill down in to the Letters folder and then the Keys folder to select the 0 sprite. Then click on the OK button. Place the sprite in the lower-left corner of the stage, as shown in Figure 8.12. Following this same process, add sprites 1 through 9 to the bottom of the stage as well. At this point, all that is left in the design of the application's user interface is the display and repositioning of the monitor, which you will do in the next step.

Step 4: Adding Variables Required by the Application

In order to execute, the Number Guessing game requires three variables, as shown in Figure 8.13. To add these variables to the application, click on the

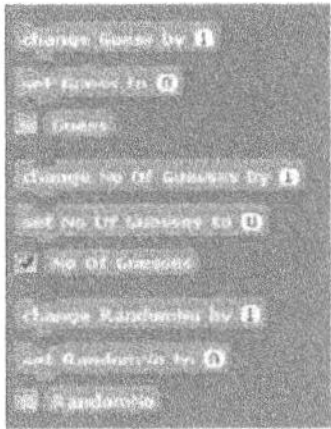

Figure 8.13
The Number Guessing game requires three variables.

Variables button located at the top of the blocks palette and then click on the Make a Variable button three times to define variables named Guess, No Of Guesses, and RandomNo.

The variable named Guess will be used to store the most recent guess made by the player. The variable named No Of Guesses will be used to keep track of the number of guesses made by the player during each game. The variable named RandomNo will be used to store the game's randomly generated secret number. Once added, clear the check box controls belonging to the Guess and No Of Guesses variables to prevent their monitors from being displayed. Lastly, drag and drop the monitor for the No Of Guesses variable to the middle right-hand side of the stage.

Step 5: Adding an Audio File to the Application

The Number Guessing game makes use of two audio files that are played as sound effects when the player makes incorrect and correct guesses. The audio file played when the player enters a missed guess is the default pop file, which is automatically included as part of each of the button sprites used in the application. The second audio file is the Fairydust file, which is played whenever the player manages to correctly guess the mystery number.

To add the Fairydust audio file, select the Cat sprite thumbnail in the sprite list and then click on the Sounds tab located at the top of the scripts area. Next, click on the Import button to display the Import Sound window, and then double-click on the Electronic folder, select the Fairydust file, and click on OK.

Step 6: Adding Scripts to Capture Player Input

The programming logic that drives the Number Guessing application is divided into a series of scripts belonging to the application's sprites. Specifically, small scripts must be added to each of the button sprites to capture and save player guesses. In addition, two scripts must be added to the Cat sprite. These two scripts, which are responsible for starting the game and processing player guesses, will be covered in Step 7.

To begin work on each of the scripts belonging to the button sprites, select the sprite representing the 0 button and then add the following code blocks to it:

The script begins with a hat block that executes whenever the sprite is clicked (when the player clicks on it as a guess). When this occurs, the second code block in the script sends a Player has guessed broadcast message to the other sprites as a signal that the player has submitted a guess. The Player has guessed must be typed into the control block exactly as shown. A third code block is then used to assign a value to the Guess variable, recording the player's guess. Note that in this example, setting Guess to 0 indicates that the player has submitted a guess of 0. The last code block in the script plays the default pop audio file, which lets the player know that the guess has been processed.

Note

A *broadcast message* is a message exchanged between sprites that signals when an event of some type has occurred within an application. Broadcast messages are generated by and received using various control code blocks, which you will learn all about in Chapter 10, "Changing the Way Sprites Look and Behave." For now, all you need to know is that this application uses broadcast messages in order to coordinate activity and keep track of what is occurring within the game.

The scripts that need to be added to the rest of the button sprites are almost identical to the script that you just added. The only difference is that you need to modify the value that is set in the third code block to properly reflect which button sprite each script belongs to. The easiest way to add these scripts to the other nine button sprites is to drag and drop an instance of the first script onto each of the nine other sprites and then to select each sprite, one at a time, and modify the value of the third code block accordingly.

Step 7: Processing Player Guesses

Once scripts have been added to all 10 of the button sprites, it is time to create the two scripts belonging to the Cat sprite. The first of these scripts is shown next and is responsible for initializing the game and getting it ready to play.

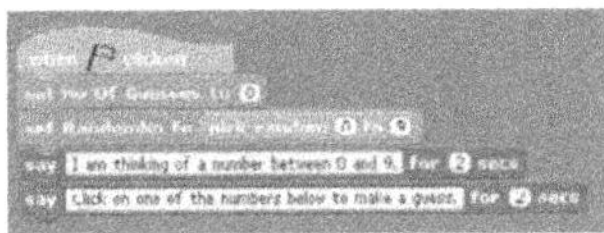

This script is executed when the player clicks on the green flag button. It begins by assigning an initial value of 0 to No Of Guesses and then assigns a randomly generated value in the range of 0 to 9 to a variable named RandomNo. Lastly, it displays a pair of messages that inform the player that the cat is thinking of a number and challenges the player to try to guess it.

The second and final script to be added to the Cat sprite is shown next. This script is automatically executed whenever the Player has guessed broadcast message is received. This happens when the player clicks on one of the 10 button sprites. First, the script modifies the value assigned to No Of Guesses by increasing it by 1. This allows the application to keep track of the number of guesses that the player has made in the current game.

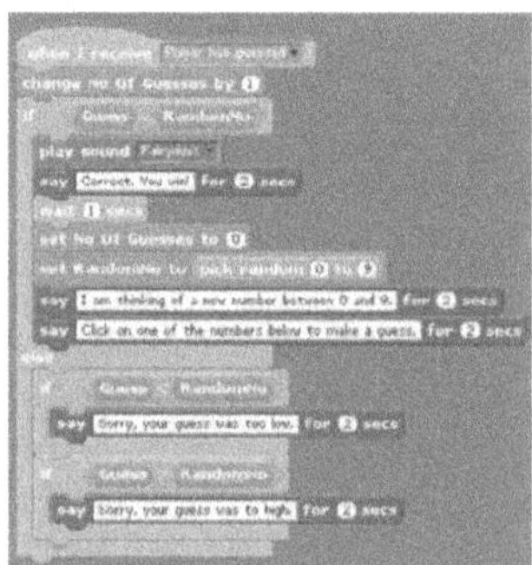

The rest of the script is made up of code blocks embedded within a control block. The control block begins by evaluating the value assigned to the Guess variable to see if it is equal to the value assigned to the RandomNo variable. If this is the case, a series of code blocks embedded within the upper portion of the control block are executed. If this is not the case, code blocks embedded in the bottom of the control block are executed.

The code statements located in the upper half of the control block, which execute when the player enters a correct guess, perform the following actions:

- Play the Fairydust audio file that was added to the Cat sprite back in Step 5
- Notify the player that the game has been won
- Pause script execution for one second
- Reset the value of No Of Guesses to 0

- Select a new random number for the game

- Challenge the player to play again

If, on the other hand, the player enters an incorrect guess, the code blocks embedded at the bottom of the script are executed. These code blocks are organized into two separate control blocks. The first control block evaluates the value assigned to Guess to see if it is less than RandomNo, and if it is, a message is displayed that informs the player that the guess was too low. The second control block determines if the value assigned to Guess is less than RandomNo, and if it is, a message is displayed that informs the player that the guess was too high.

Step 8: Saving and Executing Your New Scratch Application

At this point, you now have all the information that you need to create your own copy of the Number Guessing game. If you have not already done so, save your new Scratch project. Once saved, switch to Presentation mode, run the game, and put it through its paces. Remember to begin game play by clicking on the green flag button and following the instructions provided by the Cat sprite.

Summary

This chapter provided a thorough overview of Scratch numbers code blocks and demonstrated their usage. This included learning how to perform mathematical calculations and generate random numbers, as well as how to perform numeric comparisons. You learned how to perform different types of logical comparisons and to combine code blocks that execute logical and comparison operations to carry out advanced comparison operations. On top of all this, you learned how to perform a host of advanced mathematical operations like rounding numbers and executing different arithmetic functions. You also learned how to create another Scratch application, the Number Guessing game.

CHAPTER EIGHT

Changing Look and Behave

By its very nature, Scratch lends itself to the development of graphical applications that involve the manipulation of sprites. This includes taking actions that affect the appearance and behavior of both sprites and the stage background. Sprite and background appearance and behavior can be controlled using looks code blocks. Looks code blocks can be used to affect sprite appearance through the application of special effects, to make sprites visible or invisible as applications execute, and even to change sprite costumes and stage backgrounds. This chapter offers an in-depth overview of all of Scratch's looks code blocks and will guide you through the creation of your next Scratch project, the Crazy Eight Ball game.

The major topics covered in this chapter include:

- Learning how to programmatically change a sprite's costume

- Learning how to display text in speech and thought bubbles

- Discovering how to apply a range of special graphical effects to sprites

- Learning how to change a sprite's size

- Making sprites appear and disappear during application execution

- Specifying how sprites that overlap one another should be displayed

Changing Sprite Costumes and Backgrounds

Depending on whether you have selected a sprite's thumbnail or the stage thumbnail in the sprite list, several different code blocks are displayed when you look at Scratch's looks blocks in the blocks palette. For starters, the first three code blocks are different, as shown in Figure 10.1.

Both sets of code blocks have similar tasks, with one set focusing on working with sprite costumes while the other set is focused on working with the stage's background.

Changing Sprite Costumes

Every sprite that is added to a Scratch application is capable of changing its appearance by changing its costume. Sprites can be assigned any number of costumes and switch between them at any time. To add a costume to a sprite, all you have to do is select the sprite's thumbnail, click on the Costumes tab located at the top of the scripts area, and then click on the Import button. This opens a window that allows you to locate and select a graphic file to be used as a new costume for the sprite.

Every costume that is added to a sprite is automatically assigned a number and a name (based on the graphic's filename). The first costume in the costume list represents the sprite when the application is started. However, using drag and drop, you can rearrange the order in which costumes are listed. In addition, using the first looks block shown in Figure 10.1, you can programmatically replace a sprite's current costume by specifying the name of a different costume. For example, the following script demonstrates how to use this code block in a loop to repeatedly change a sprite's costume 10 times at half-second intervals. The result is the generation of animation that makes it look like the bat is flying.

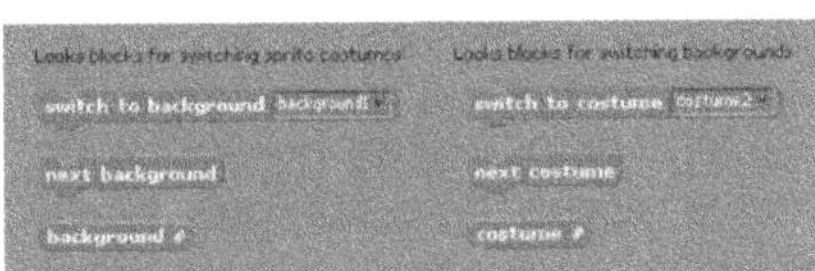

Figure 10.1
The code blocks on the left are displayed when you are working with a sprite, and the code blocks on the right are displayed when you are working with the stage.

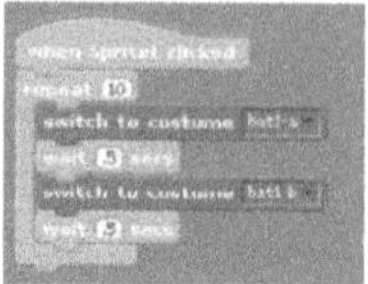

To change the costume of the sprite to which this script is added, select the costume's name from the looks block's drop-down list. The block's drop-down list is automatically populated with a list of all of the costumes that have been added to the sprite. The costumes listed in the previous example refer to two costumes representing different views of a bat, as shown in Figure 10.2, and are supplied as part of a collection of graphic files that ships with Scratch.

Costume numbers are automatically assigned by Scratch as you import new costumes into a sprite. The first costume assigned to a sprite is given a costume number of 1. Each successive costume is assigned a higher number, as demonstrated in Figure 10.3.

Using the second looks block shown on the left-hand side of Figure 10.1, you can change a sprite's costume to the next costume in the costume list. For example, the following script automatically changes a sprite's costume whenever the sprite is clicked.

When executed, the script changes the sprite's costume to the next costume in the list. By clicking on the sprite repeatedly, you continue changing the sprite's

Figure 10.2
Bat costumes.

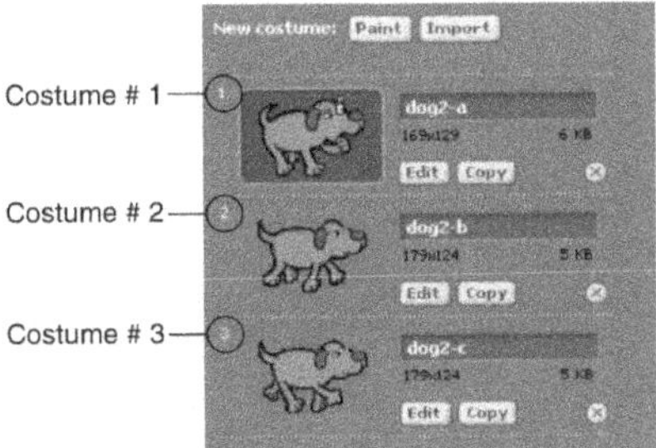

Costume # 1
Costume # 2
Costume # 3

Figure 10.3
Three costumes have been added to a sprite, each of which depicts a slightly different version of a blue dog. These costumes are numbered 1, 2, and 3 and are named dog2-a, dog2-b, and dog2-c, respectively.

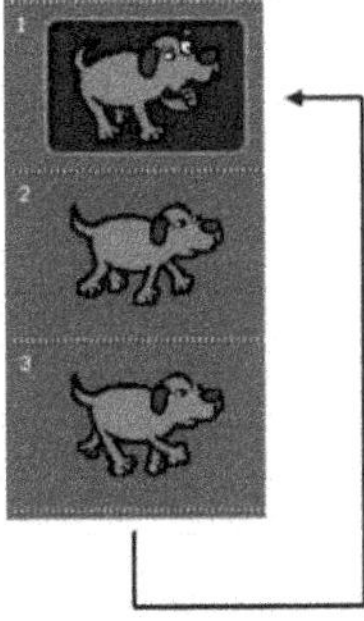

Figure 10.4
Scratch loops back to the beginning of the sprite's costume list as necessary to fulfill additional costume switches.

costume. Once the last costume in the costume list has been displayed, Scratch will go back to the top of the costume list and start over, as depicted in Figure 10.4.

The last looks block shown at bottom left of Figure 10.1 can be used to display a monitor that presents a sprite costume number on the stage. Alternatively, you can use this code block as input to any code block that accepts numeric input.

Changing a Stage's Background Costumes

The looks code blocks on the right-hand side of Figure 10.1 are used to change the stage's background and work identically to their counterparts that deal with costumes. For example, the following script demonstrates how to randomly set the stage's background to one of three options.

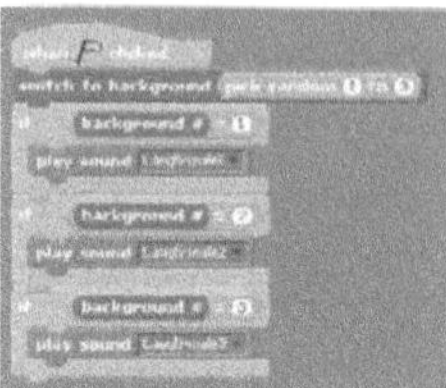

Note that in addition to changing the stage's background twice, this example also plays one of three audio files, depending on which of the three backgrounds is randomly selected.

Making Sprites Talk and Think

The following set of looks code blocks, shown in Figure 10.5, is applicable only to sprites and can used to display text in speech and thought bubbles, making a sprite look like it is talking or thinking.

Figure 10.6 provides examples of how speech and thought bubbles look.

The first two code blocks are used to display text in speech bubbles. The difference between these two code blocks is that the first code block displays its text

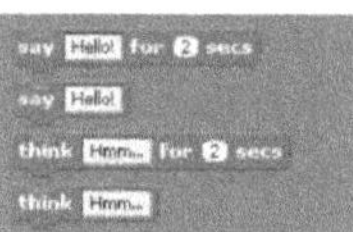

Figure 10.5
Using these code blocks, you can display text in both speech and thought bubbles.

Figure 10.6
Speech and thought bubbles resemble callouts used to display captions in cartoons found in many popular newspaper comic strips.

for a specified number of seconds, and the second code block permanently displays its text (until the text is overridden by another speech or thought bubble). For example, the following script could be used to display the text Hello! for two seconds in a speech bubble.

Tip

Any text displayed using the second and fourth code blocks shown in Figure 10.5 do not automatically go away. However, you can clear out the text displayed in a speech or thought bubble by executing a speech or thought code block with no text typed in it.

Similarly, the following script demonstrates how to display a text message of Hmm... in a thought bubble.

Applying Special Effects to Costumes and Backgrounds

The next three looks code blocks, shown in Figure 10.7, apply to both sprites and the stage and can be used to apply and clear different graphical special effects.

The first and second code blocks shown in Figure 10.7 select and then apply one of the following special effects to a sprite's costume or to the stage's background.

- **Color.** Modifies the costume or background's color.

- **Fisheye.** Magnifies a portion of a costume or background.

- **Whirl.** Twists and distorts a portion of a costume or background.

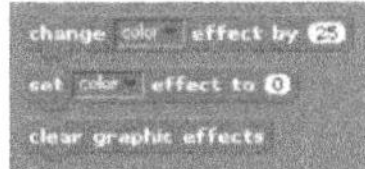

Figure 10.7
These code blocks allow you to set and clear different graphics effects on sprites.

- **Pixelate.** Displays a sprite or background at a lower resolution than the resolution at which the image was created.

- **Mosaic.** Creates an image made up of repeated instances of a sprite or background.

- **Brightness.** Modifies an image by increasing or decreasing its intensity of light.

- **Ghost.** Fades the appearance of a costume or background to make it look transparent.

An example of each of these graphic effects on a sprite is shown in Figure 10.8.

To develop a better understanding of how to work with these two code blocks, let's look at a couple of examples. In this first example, a sprite's appearance is changed by executing a loop four times. Each time the loop executes, it applies the ghost effect to the sprite to which it belongs.

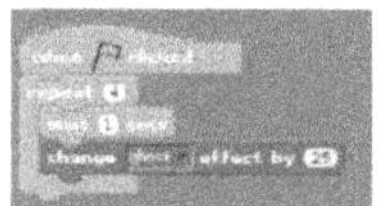

Note that the value specified in the input field for the code block in the previous script is 25, which represents a percentage value. As such, for each of the four times that the loop repeats, the sprite fades away until at the end of the last execution of the loop, the sprite completely disappears.

Figure 10.8
A demonstration of how special effects affect a sprite.

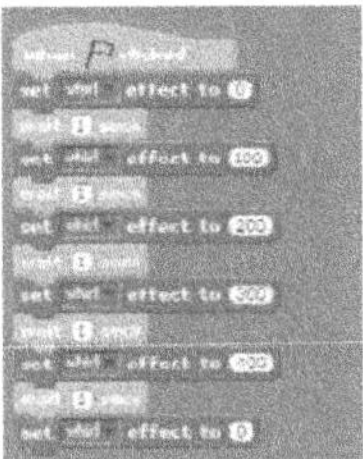

This second example applies the whirl special effect to its sprite. Specifically, it begins by clearing any previous whirl effect that may have been applied to the sprite. Then, over a period of four seconds, it slowly modifies the appearance of the sprite by applying an increased application of the whirl effect. A one-second pause then ensues, and the sprite is returned to its original state.

The last looks code block restores a costume or background back to its original appearance regardless of how many different graphical effects may have been applied to it. For example, the following statement demonstrates how to restore a costume or background's appearance when the green flag button is pressed.

Changing a Sprite's Size

The next three looks code block, shown in Figure 10.9, apply only to sprites. They allow you to change a sprite's size.

The first code block modifies a sprite's size by specifying a relative value. Using this code block, as demonstrated next, you can slowly increase a sprite's size and then reduce its size just as quickly.

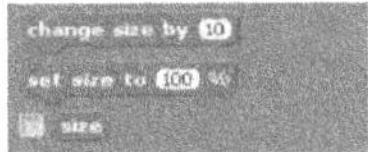

Figure 10.9
With these code blocks, you can modify a sprite's size.

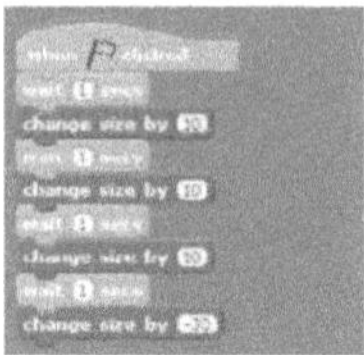

The second code block shown in Figure 10.9 lets you set a sprite's size to a specific percentage of its current size (larger or smaller). For example, the following script begins by doubling the size of a sprite. It then pauses for a second and reduces the sprite to 50% of its original size. After another brief pause, the sprite is restored to its original size.

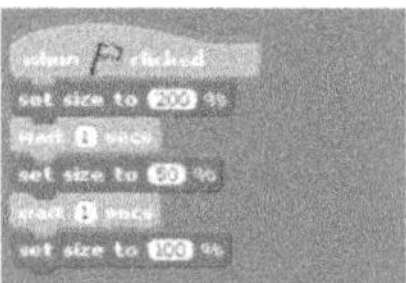

Making Sprites Appear and Disappear

The next two looks code blocks, shown in Figure 10.10, apply only to sprites. As the text displayed on the blocks indicates, they programmatically display or hide a sprite.

Since they do not accept any input, these two code blocks are very easy to work with. For example, the following script can be added to any sprite to make it disappear and then reappear after a one-second pause.

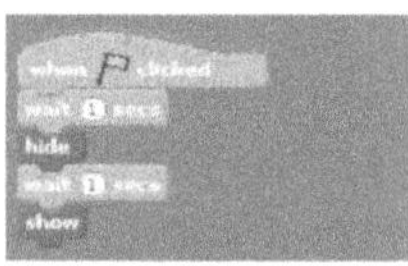

Figure 10.10
With these two code blocks, you can control when sprites appear on the stage.

Determining What Happens when Two Sprites Overlap

The last two Scratch looks code blocks, shown in Figure 10.11, specify what happens when all or part of a sprite is covered by another sprite.

In Scratch, each sprite that you add to an application is assigned to a layer. For example, suppose you create an application with multiple sprites. When you add the first sprite to the application, it is placed at the topmost layer. When you add the application's second sprite, it gets added to the top layer, and the previous sprite gets moved back one layer. Each additional sprite starts off on the top layer and stays there until you either add another new sprite or until you click on one of the sprites that was previously added, which moves the selected sprite back to the topmost layer.

By default, the first sprite would be placed on the top layer. The second sprite added to the application would be placed on the second layer, and the third sprite would be placed on the third layer.

Understanding the layer on which a sprite has been placed is important because the sprite's layer assignment determines whether it remains on top or is displayed underneath another sprite when they overlap one another. Sprites at higher levels remain on top of sprites at lower levels.

N o t e

> To better understand the importance of levels, consider what happens when you place five pieces of paper on top of one another on a desk. The piece of paper sitting on top (at the top layer) is visible, and your view of the other pieces of paper is obstructed. Now, reach into the middle of the stack of paper, pull out a sheet, and place it on top of all the other pages. By altering the page's layer position, you have now made it visible.

In addition to controlling what happens to sprites by adding them to applications in a specific order, controlling their layer position, you can use the code blocks shown in Figure 10.12 to programmatically control a sprite layer location. For example, using the first code block, you can move a sprite to the top layer, ensuring that it remains visible at all times on the stage, even when other sprites come into contact with it.

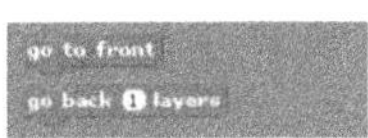

Figure 10.11
With these code blocks, you can determine what happens when two sprites overlap.

As an example of how to work with both of these code blocks, revisit the Ball Chase game that was presented in Chapter 9, where both of these two code blocks were used to ensure that end of game messages were displayed on top of all other sprites. In addition, the application also used these blocks to ensure that the cat overlaps the ball when it catches it.

Developing the Crazy Eight Ball Game

Now it is time to turn your attention to the development of a new Scratch application, the Crazy Eight Ball game. This game simulates the operation of a crazy eight ball fortune-telling toy. As you work on the development of this game, you will get additional experience with different looks code blocks. In total, the application is made up of three sprites and three scripts. Figure 10.12 shows how the game looks when first started.

To play the game, think of a question and then click on the image of the cat located in the center of the eight ball. Once clicked, the image of the cat is replaced with an 8, as demonstrated in Figure 10.13, and over the next four seconds, the sounds of bubbles can be heard.

Figure 10.12
To play, you must ask questions that can be answered with yes/no-style answers.

Figure 10.13
It takes a few moments for the crazy eight ball to come up with an answer.

Figure 10.14
The crazy eight ball has decided not to answer the player's question.

The crazy eight ball displays any of five randomly selected answers in response to player questions. The range of answers supported by the game includes:

- Maybe!

- No!

- Yes!

- Ask a different question!

- Maybe… but then maybe not!

Figure 10.14 shows how the game looks once it has finally decided on an answer to the player's question.

The development of this application project will be created by following a series of steps, as outlined here:

1. Creating a new Scratch application project.

2. Adding and removing sprites.

3. Adding the variable needed by the application.

4. Adding an audio file to the application.

5. Adding a script to control the display of the 8 in the eight ball.

6. Adding the programming logic required to operate the eight ball.

7. Saving and executing your work.

Step 1: Creating a New Scratch Project

Begin the creation of the Crazy Eight Ball game by creating a new Scratch project. The easiest way is to start Scratch, which automatically creates a new application project. Alternatively, if Scratch is already open, create a new application by clicking on the New button located on the Scratch menu bar.

Step 2: Adding and Removing Sprites

The Crazy Eight Ball game consists of three sprites and three scripts, as shown in Figure 10.15.

The first sprite that you need to add to the game is that of an empty eight ball. The second sprite is that of a number 8. You will find copies of graphics for both of these sprites located on this book's companion CD-ROM. You can add these sprites to your new Scratch application by clicking on the Choose New Sprite from File button and then selecting these files. Alternatively, you can create them yourself by clicking on the Paint New Sprite button and then using the Paint Editor program. Once added to the stage, reposition these two sprites so that the eight ball is centered in the middle of the stage and the number is centered in the middle of the eight ball.

The application's third sprite is that of a cat's face. You can create this sprite by using the Paint Editor program to edit the application's default sprite, removing the Cat sprite's body, leaving just its face in place. Once modified, click on the

Figure 10.15
An overview of the different components that make up the Crazy Eight Ball game.

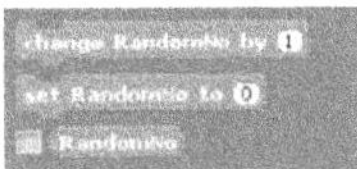

Figure 10.16
The Crazy Eight Ball game requires one variable.

Grow Sprite button located on Scratch's toolbar and then click on the image of the Cat sprite 12 times to increase the size of the cat's face. Next, reposition the Cat sprite, moving it onto the center of the eight ball so that it overlaps the Cat sprite. At this point, the overall design of the Crazy Eight Ball game is complete.

Before moving on to the next step, rename these three sprites Cat, EightBall, and Number, as shown in Figure 10.15.

Step 3: Adding a Variable Required by the Application

In order to execute, the Crazy Eight Ball game requires the definition of the variable shown in Figure 10.16. To add this variable, click on the Variables button located at the top of the blocks palette, click on the Make a Variable button, and create a new variable named RandomNo.

This variable will be used to store a randomly generated number that the game will use when generating answers to player questions.

Step 4: Adding an Audio File to the Application

The Crazy Eight Ball game makes use of a single sound effect, which sounds like bubbles being blown in water. This sound is played for four seconds preceding the display of the eight ball's answer. The audio file that is played must be added to the Cat sprite. To add this sound file, select the Cat sprite thumbnail in the sprite list and then click on the Sounds tab located at the top of the scripts area. Next, click on the Import button to display the Import Sound window, double-click on the Effects folder, select the Bubbles audio file, and then click on OK.

Step 5: Creating a Script to Control the Display of the 8 in the Eight Ball

Of the application's three scripts, two belong to the Number sprite. These scripts, shown next, are automatically executed based on the receipt of broadcast messages.

Specifically, when a message of Show 8 is received, the Eight sprite is made visible. When the message Hide 8 is received, the Eight sprite is hidden. The receipt of these messages serves as triggers, which control when the Eight sprite is visible (which only occurs when the eight ball is in the process of preparing to generate an answer).

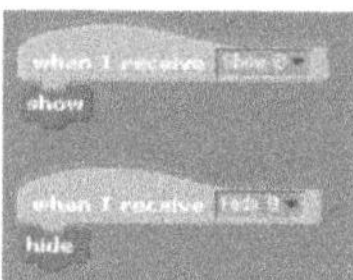

As you can see, these two scripts each use a looks code block to control sprite visibility. Since the game begins by displaying only the image of the Cat sprite, go ahead and click on the second script belonging to the Eight sprite, hiding it from view.

Step 6: Adding the Programming Logic Needed to Control the Eight Ball

The last script in the application, shown next, belongs to the Cat sprite. It is executed whenever the player thinks of a question and clicks on the Cat sprite for an answer.

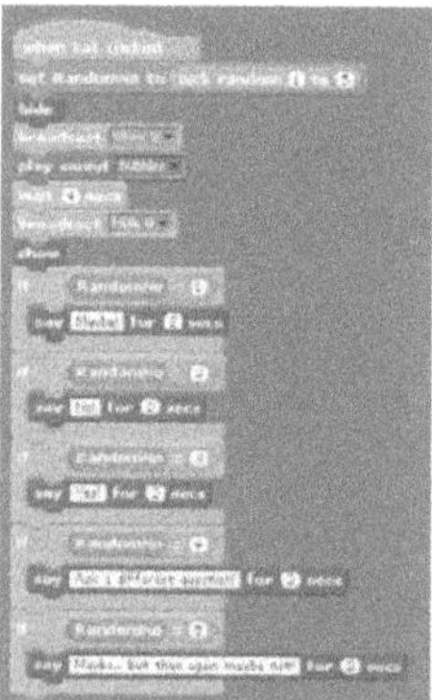

Once started, the script begins by assigning a random number in the range of 1 to 5 to the RandomNo variable. Next, a looks code block is executed, hiding the Cat sprite and then the broadcast message Show 8 is sent. This message will trigger the execution of a script belonging to the `Eight` sprite. Next, the `Bubbles` audio file is played, and the script's execution is paused for four seconds, allowing Scratch time to finish playing the audio file. Once the four seconds is up, a second broadcast message of `Hide 8` is sent, triggering the hiding of the `Eight` sprite.

Next, the `Cat` sprite is redisplayed on the stage and the value assigned to `RandomNo` is analyzed. Depending on the value assigned to `RandomNo`, one of five different text messages is displayed in a speech bubble. After two seconds, the bubble is closed, and the game waits on the player to ask another question.

Step 7: Saving and Executing Your Scratch Project

At this point, you have all of the information you need to create your own copy of the Crazy Eight Ball game. As long as you followed along carefully with the instructions provided in this chapter, you should not run into any problems. If you have not done so yet, save your new Scratch application project and then switch over to Presentation mode and test it.

Summary

In this chapter, you learned how to work with Scratch's looks code blocks. This included learning how to switch between sprite costumes and different stage backgrounds and how to apply a range of special effects to sprites and backgrounds. You learned how to display text in speech and thought bubbles, control the size of sprites, and programmatically control sprite visibility. You also learned about the importance of understanding layering and how it affects the display of sprites. This chapter also guided you through the creation of the Crazy Eight Ball game.

CHAPTER NINE

Glossary

Actor. A term used to refer to sprites and the role they play as they interact with one another on the stage.

Animated GIF. A graphic is made up of two or more frames, each of which is displayed as an automated sequence when the GIF file is displayed.

Boolean. A term used to represent data that has either of two values, true or false.

Brightness. The application or restriction of the intensity of light in a graphic image.

Broadcast Message. An electronic message sent between sprites as a means of coordinating application activity.

Code Block. A graphical command used in the creation of a script.

Collision. An event that occurs whenever two sprites come into contact with one another on the stage.

Compression. The process of reducing the size of sound and graphics files in order to reduce the overall size of Scratch applications.

Conditional Logic. The process of executing sets of code blocks based on whether or not a tested condition proves true.

Costumes. Images that are used to represent a sprite on the stage.

Data. A piece of information collected, stored, modified, and processed during application execution.

Debugger. A program or utility that can be used to execute an application within a special environment that allows programmers to slow and monitor the execution of an application's script as it runs.

Decimal. A floating point or real number.

Endless Loop. A loop that does not have a means for terminating its execution.

Event Handling. The process of initiating script execution based on the occurrence of predefined events, such as a mouse click, the pressing of a keyboard key, or the clicking of a sprite.

Fisheye. A graphic effect that can be applied to a sprite or background in order to magnify a portion of its image.

Ghost. A graphic effect that fades the appearance of a costume or background, making it look transparent.

Global Variable. A variable that can be modified by any script in an application.

Gradient. A color created by blending together the foreground and background colors.

Hat Block. A code block that creates event-driven scripts.

IDE (Integrated Development Environment). A graphical application development environment designed to facilitate program development.

Integer. An absolute or whole number that does not have a decimal point.

Java. A popular web-based programming language that is a prerequisite for executing a Scratch application on the Scratch website.

Local Variable. A variable that can be modified only by scripts belonging to the sprite in which the variable is defined.

Logical Error. An error created by a mistake made by the programmer when developing the logic implemented by a script.

Looks Blocks. Code blocks that affect sprite and background appearance and display text.

Loop. A collection of one or more code blocks that are repeatedly executed.

Monitor. A small block that displays the value currently assigned to the code block.

Mosaic. A special graphic effect that creates an image made up of repeated instances of a sprite or background.

Motion Blocks. Code blocks that control sprite placement, direction, rotation, and movement.

MP3. An audio file that utilizes advanced compression technology while retaining high audio quality.

Nest. The process of embedding one set of code blocks within another set of code blocks.

Numbers Blocks. Code blocks that perform mathematical operations, logical comparisons, rounding, and other arithmetic operations.

Order of Precedence. The set of rules that is followed when evaluating a numeric expression.

Paint Editor. A Scratch program that supports the creation of graphics files to be used as the basis for creating and modifying sprites and backgrounds.

Pen. A virtualized drawing tool that can be used to draw on the stage.

Pen Blocks. Code blocks that can be used to draw using different colors and pen sizes.

Pixelate. A special graphic effect that displays a sprite or background at a lower resolution than the resolution at which it was created.

Project. A collection of sprites, scripts, backgrounds, and sounds that is used as the basis for creating Scratch applications.

Real Number. A number that includes a decimal number.

Reporter Block. A code block that has either rounded or angled sides and is specifically designed as a mechanism for providing input for other code blocks to process.

Rotation Center. The point on a sprite that remains in position when a sprite is rotated.

Run-time Error. An application error that occurs when an application attempts to perform an illegal action.

Scope. A term that refers to the area within an application where a variable's value can be accessed and modified.

Scratch Board. A special piece of hardware that you can buy from the Scratch website and attach to your computer in order to collect and process environmental and user-provided input.

Scratch Cards. PDF files that you can print and use as a quick reference for performing certain tasks.

Script. A collection of code blocks that outlines the programming logic that influences the operation of a sprite.

Sensing Blocks. Code blocks that can be used to determine the location of the mouse-pointer, its distance from other sprites, and whether a sprite is touching another sprite.

Sound Blocks. Code blocks that control the playback and volume of musical notes and audio files.

Sprite. A two-dimensional image drawn on a transparent background that can be moved around the stage. You can change its appearance using different costumes.

Squeak. A cross-platform programming language used to develop Scratch.

Stack Blocks. Code blocks with a notch at the top or a bump at the bottom that can be snapped together with other bocks to define a script's programming logic.

Stacks. Another term for a script.

Stage. The background area on the Scratch IDE upon which sprites are displayed during application execution.

String. A set of characters that can be displayed within thought and speech bubbles.

Tempo. A measurement of the speed, in beats per minute, at which a drum or note is played.

Troubleshooting. The identification, location, and elimination of programming errors, or bugs, that prevent applications from executing properly.

Variable. A location in memory where an individual piece of data is stored.

Variable Scope. Identifies the location within an application where the variable's value can be modified.

Variables Blocks. Code blocks that can be used to store data used by applications when they execute.

Wave. A file with a .wav extension that supports the storage and playback of audio files.

Whirl. A special graphic effect that twists and distorts a portion of a costume or background.

Help Book

learn creative projects with scratch
HELP BOOK
GET A BRIEF OF WHAT YOU LEARNT
BEST LEARNING BOOKLET
Best of The Best

1 Start Moving

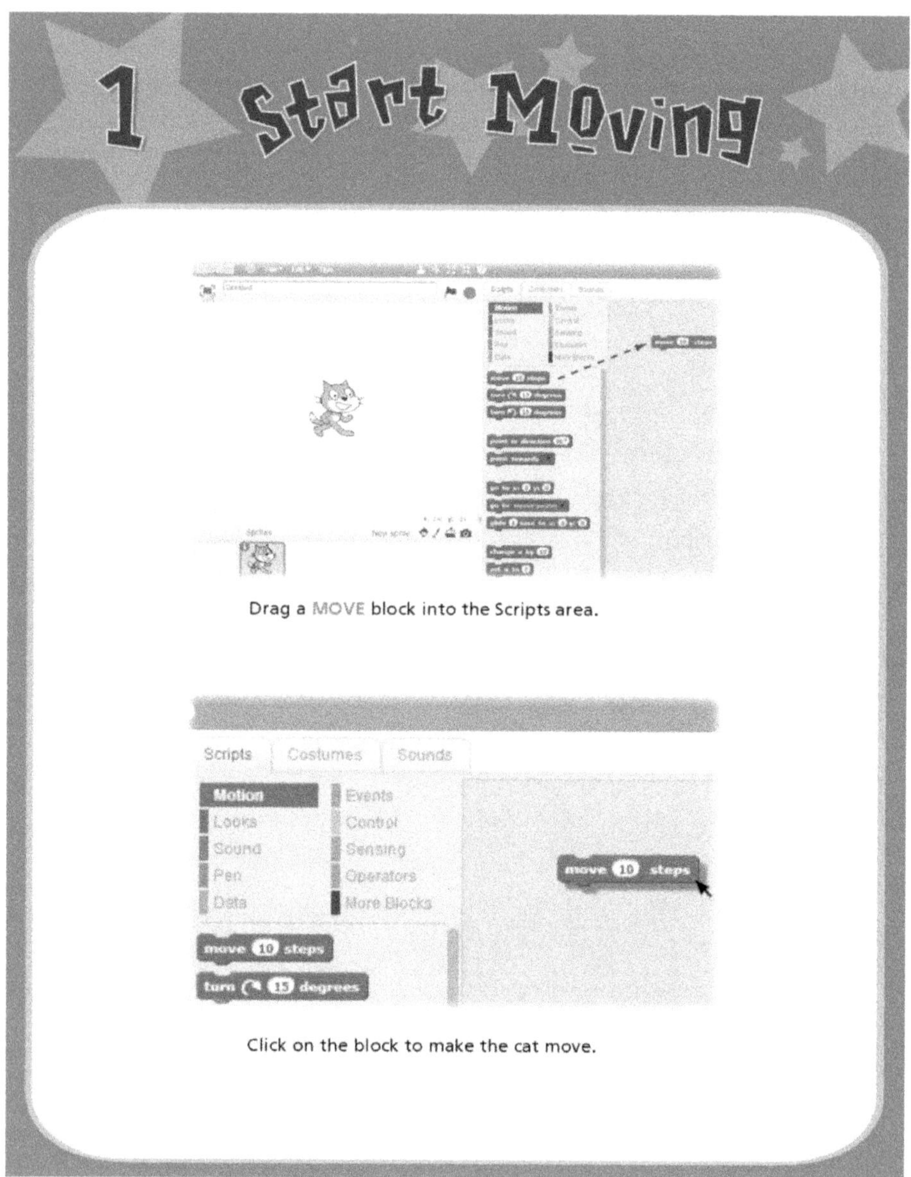

Drag a MOVE block into the Scripts area.

Click on the block to make the cat move.

2 Add a Sound

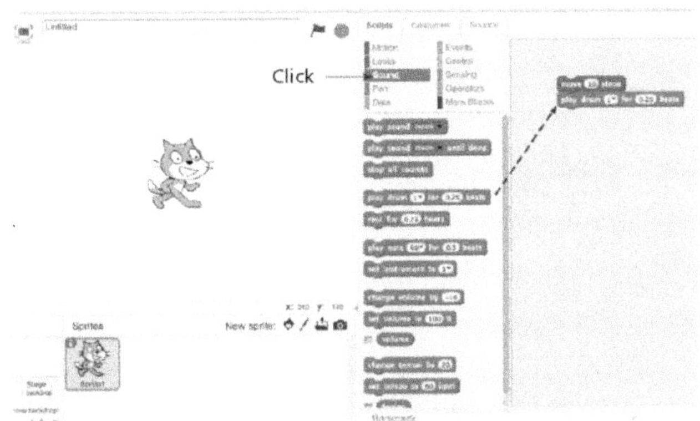

Drag out a PLAY DRUM and snap it onto the MOVE block.

Click and listen.

If you can't hear it, check that the sound on your computer is on.

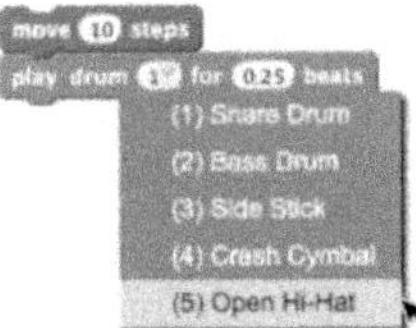

You can choose different drums from the pull-down menu.

3 Start a Dance

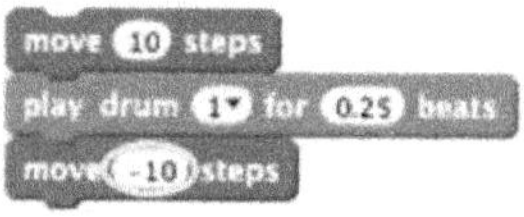

Add another MOVE block. Click inside the block and type in a minus sign.

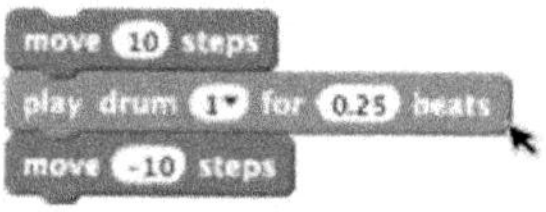

Click on any of the blocks to run the stack.

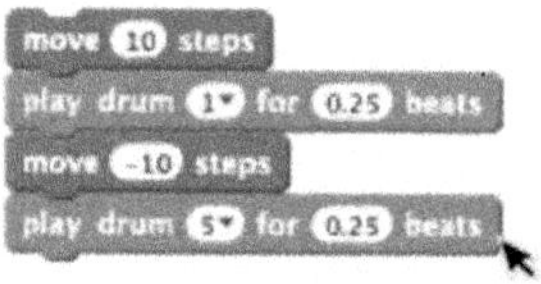

Add another PLAY DRUM block, then choose a drum from the menu. Click to run.

4 Again and Again

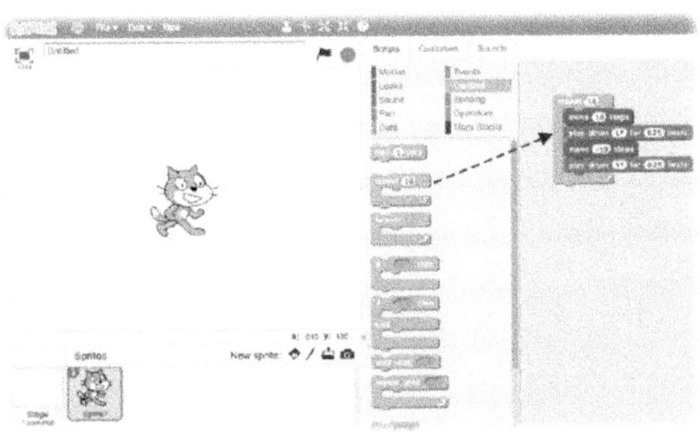

Drag out a REPEAT block and drop it on top of the stack.
You want the mouth of the REPEAT to wrap around the other blocks.

To drag a stack, pick it up from the top block.

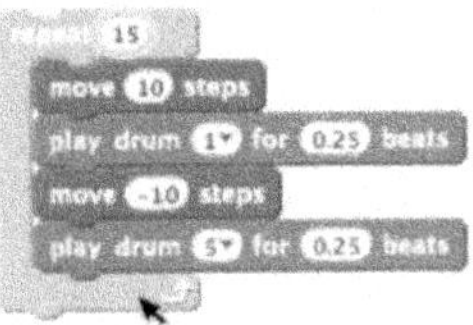

You can change how many
times it repeats.

Click to run.

*You can click on any block
to run a stack.*

5 Say Something

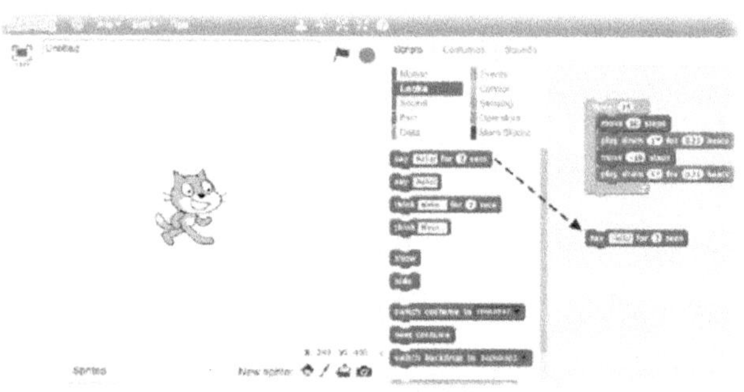

Click the **LOOKS** category and drag out a **SAY** block.

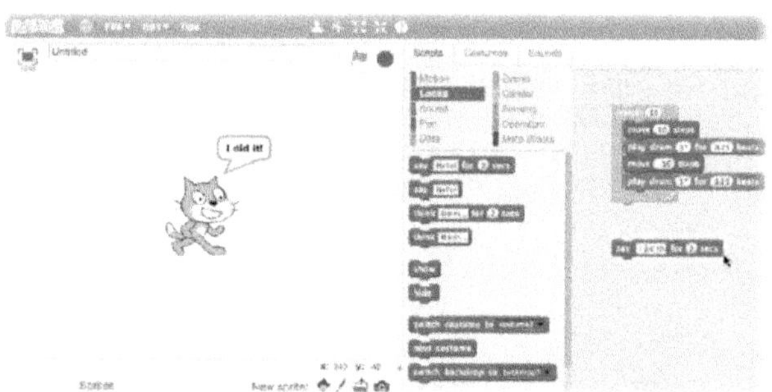

Click inside the **SAY** block and type to change the words. Click to try it.

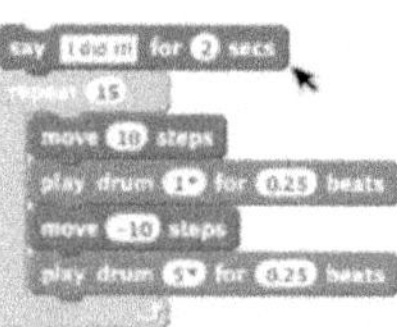

Then snap the **SAY** block on the top.

6 Green Flag

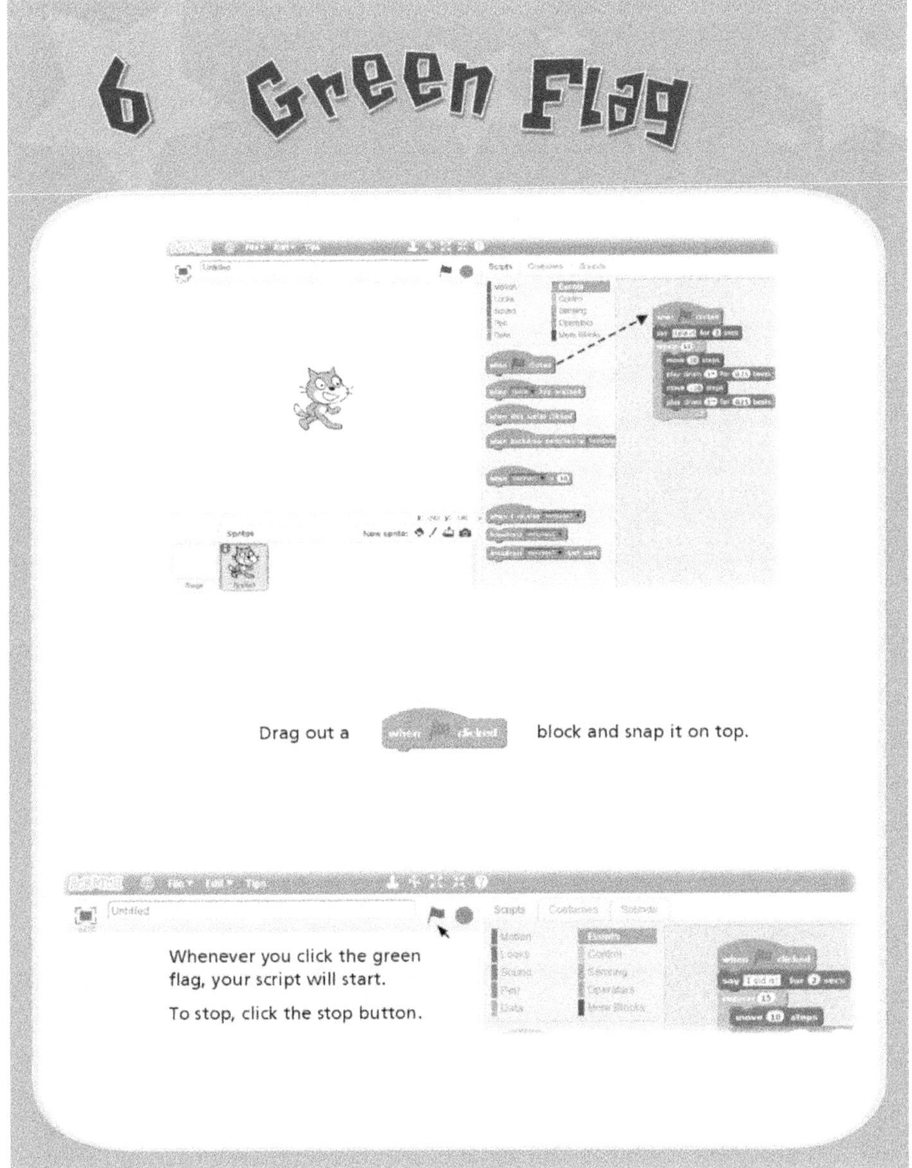

Drag out a   block and snap it on top.

Whenever you click the green flag, your script will start.

To stop, click the stop button.

7 Change Color

Now try something different...

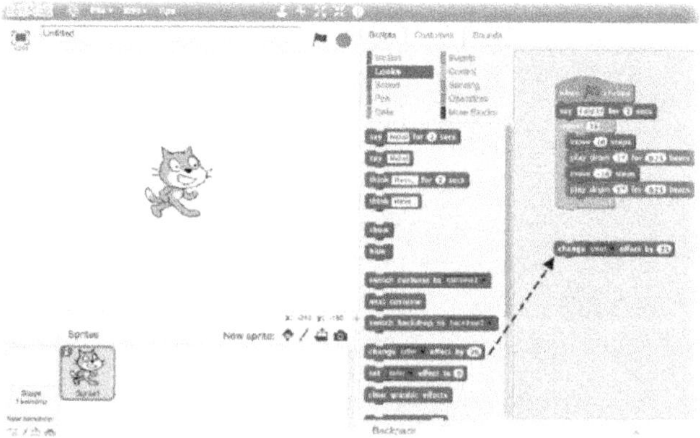

Drag out a **CHANGE EFFECT** block.

change color ▾ effect by **25**

Click to see what it does.

8 Key Press

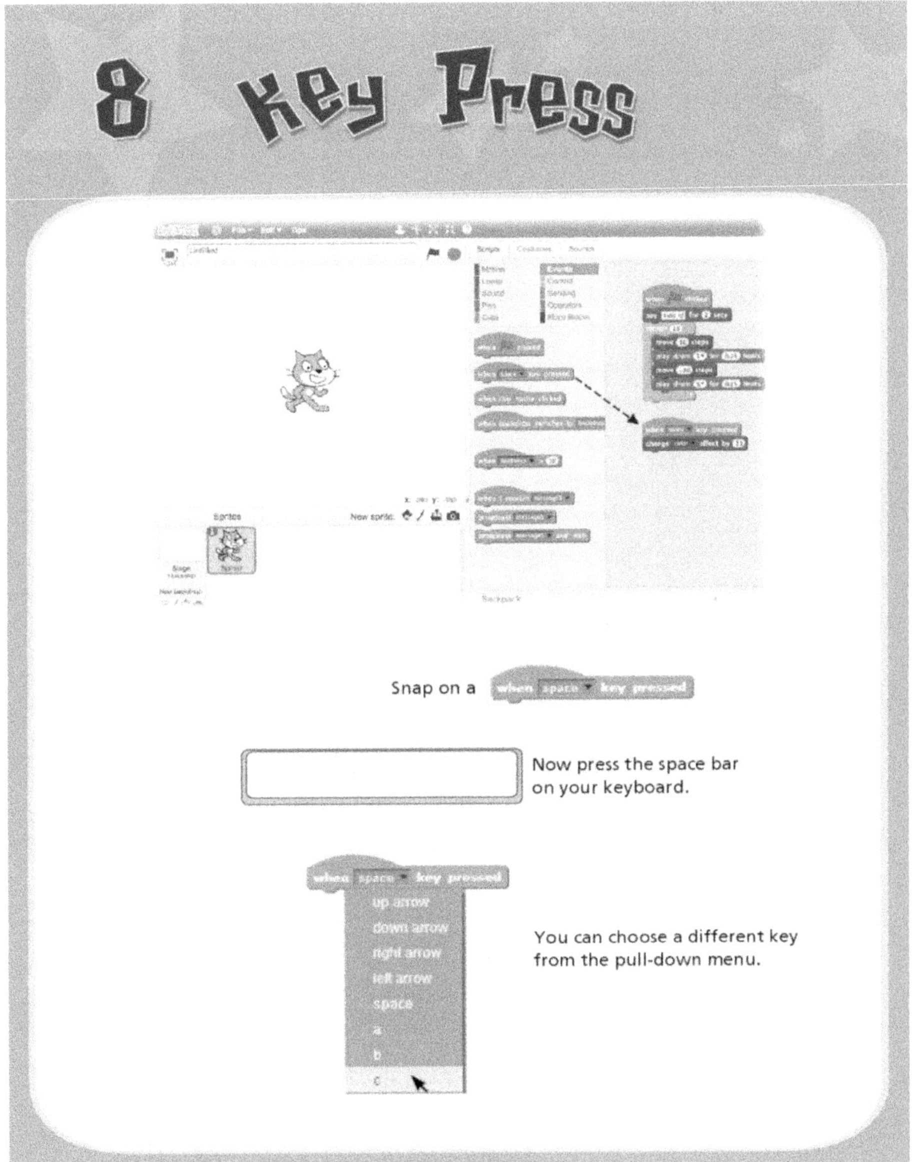

Snap on a

Now press the space bar
on your keyboard.

You can choose a different key
from the pull-down menu.

9 Add a Backdrop

You can add a backdrop to the Stage.

Click 🖼 to choose a new backdrop. ⟶

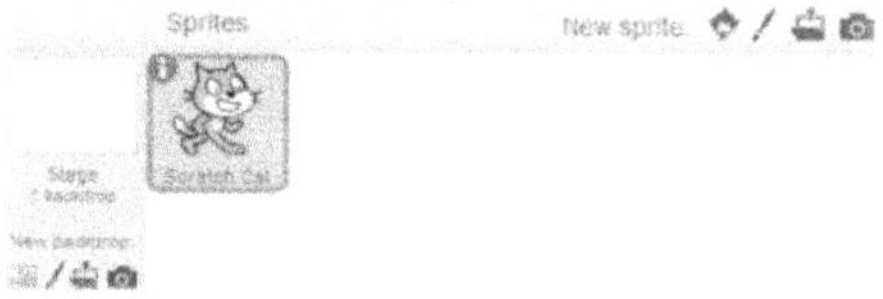

Choose a backdrop from the library (such as "Spotlight-Stage").

Click OK.

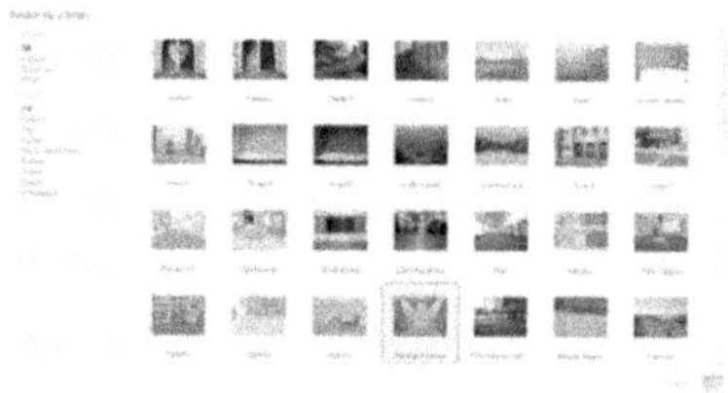

The new backdrop now appears on the Stage.

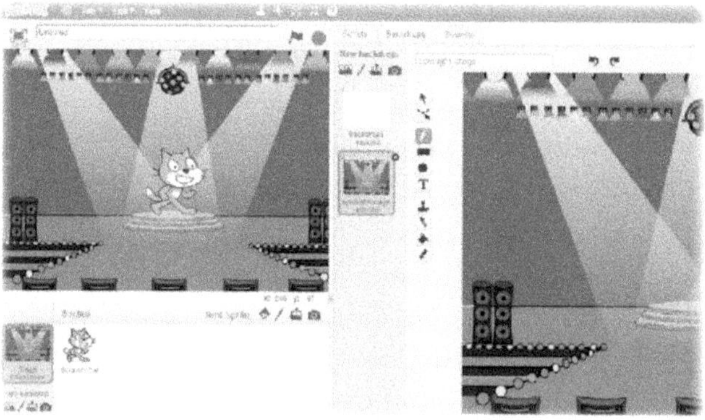

10 Add a Sprite

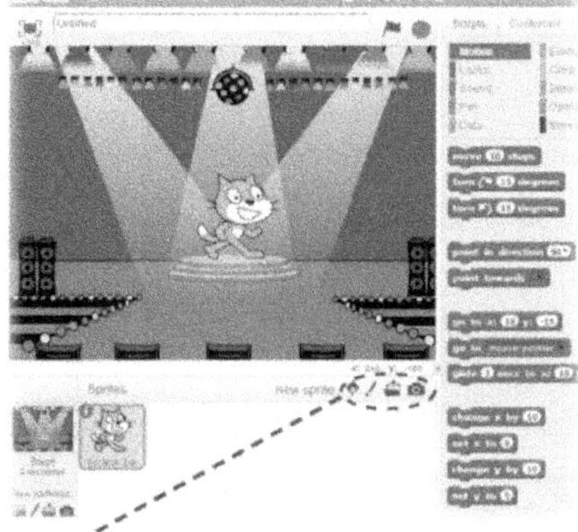

Each object in Scratch is called a sprite.

To add a new sprite, click one of these buttons.

NEW SPRITE BUTTONS:

Choose from the library

Paint your own sprite

Upload your own image or sprite

Take a picture (from a webcam)

To add this sprite, click ♦ then click **People** and select "Cassy Dance."

You can drag the characters to where you want them.

11 Explore!

Now you can tell the sprite what to do. Try the following, or explore on your own.

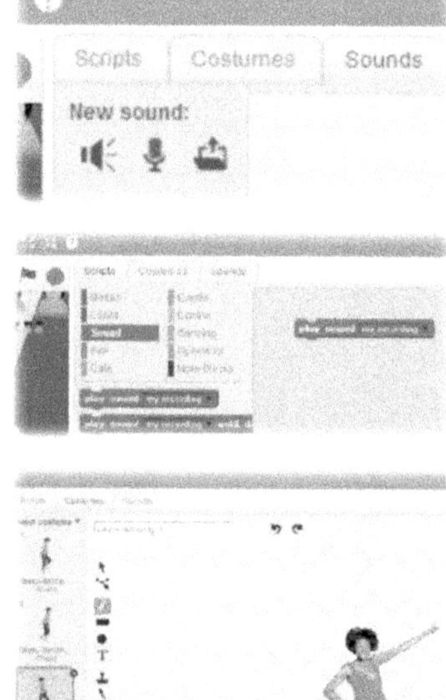

ADD SOUND

Click the **SOUNDS** tab.

You can **Choose** a sound

Record your own sound

Or **Import** a sound file.
(MP3, AIF, or WAV format)

Then, click the **SCRIPTS** tab,
and drag in a PLAY SOUND block.

Choose your sound from
the pull-down menu.

CHANGE COSTUMES

Each sprite can have more than
one costume.

To change the current costume,
click the **COSTUMES** tab.

Then click on a different costume
for the sprite.

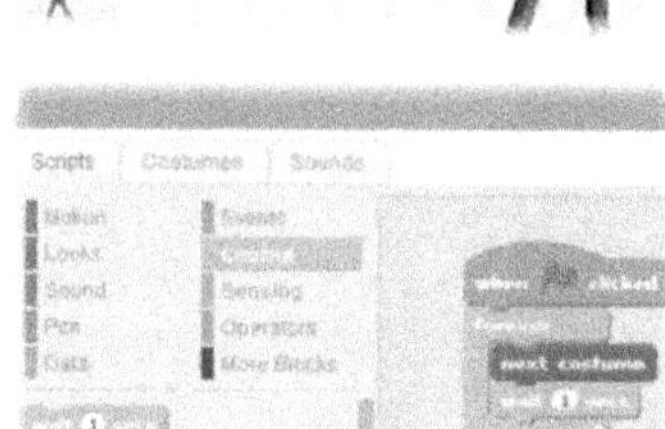

ANIMATE

You can animate a sprite by
switching between costumes.

Click the **SCRIPTS** tab.

Create a script that switches
between costumes.

12 TiPS!

Type a title for your project.

For more ideas, click **Tips**:

The **Tips Window** shows example – – – – – scripts you can use in your project.

It also explains what each of the blocks in SCRATCH does.

Save and Share

To save your project online, make sure to sign in. 

(If you want to save the file to your computer drive, click the **File** menu and choose "Download to your computer.")

When you are ready, click **See project page**

Project Page

Click [□] for full screen viewing.

Click Share for others to see and play with your project.

Type in notes about your project.

When you share, others can visit and interact with your project.

Now what? You can Create a new project or Explore for ideas.

To find out more, click Help or go to http://scratch.mit.edu/help

• 179 •

PROJECTS

1. MAKE A PING PONG GAME.
2. PROGRAM A TREX GAME.
3. MAKE A SHOOTING GAME TO SHOT THE ENEMEY.
4. MAKE A FLAPPY BIRD GAME.
5. MAKE A FOOTBAL GAME ON SCRATCH.
6. MAKE CRICKET GAME ON SCRATCH.
7. MAKE A SPRITE DANCE ON STAGE WITH MUSIC.

ENJOY LEARNING!

By! By!

You are now trained for all of the basic things!

Now you have learnt all the basics in this field you can learn more in the coming part of this series till then make projects to increase your value not to earn money thankyou!

See You In Next Part

A SMALL CREATION BY-MAYANK'KASANA